Atlantic Modern

The Architecture of the Atlantic Provinces 1950-2000

Edited by Steven Mannell

Atlantic Modern:

The Architecture of the Atlantic Provinces 1950-2000

Catalogue of the Exhibition at the Faculty of Architecture, Dalhousie University, 5410 Spring Garden Road, Halifax, Nova Scotia, May 30 - June 20, 2001. Opening: May 30, on the occasion of the 2001 RAIC Festival of Architecture. Exhibition also presented at the Art Gallery of Newfoundland and Labrador, Arts and Culture Centre, St. John's, Newfoundland, November 17, 2002 - January 5, 2003.

Editor: Steven Mannell
Catalogue Design and Production: Jennifer Uegama, Steven Mannell
Printing: Friesens

National Library of Canada Cataloguing in Publication
Main entry under title:
Atlantic modern : the architecture of the Atlantic Provinces, 1950-2000 / Steven Mannell (ed.).

ISBN 0-929112-47-4

1. Architecture--Atlantic Provinces--20th century--Exhibitions.
I. Mannell, Steven II. Title.

NA746.A8A84 2002   720'.9715'074   C2002-901383-6

Cover image and image at start of each chapter (clockwise from top left):
Holy Redeemer Catholic Church (Alfred Hennessey collection), Beth-El Synagogue (photo: Tootons; Angus Campbell collection), Sexton Memorial Gymnasium (photo: Maurice Crosby; Dalhousie University Archives), Blue Cross Centre (Architects Four Ltd.)
Title page image: View of exhibition, Faculty of Architecture, Dalhousie University, Halifax, Nova Scotia. May 30 - June 20, 2001. Photographer: Ken Kam.

Contents

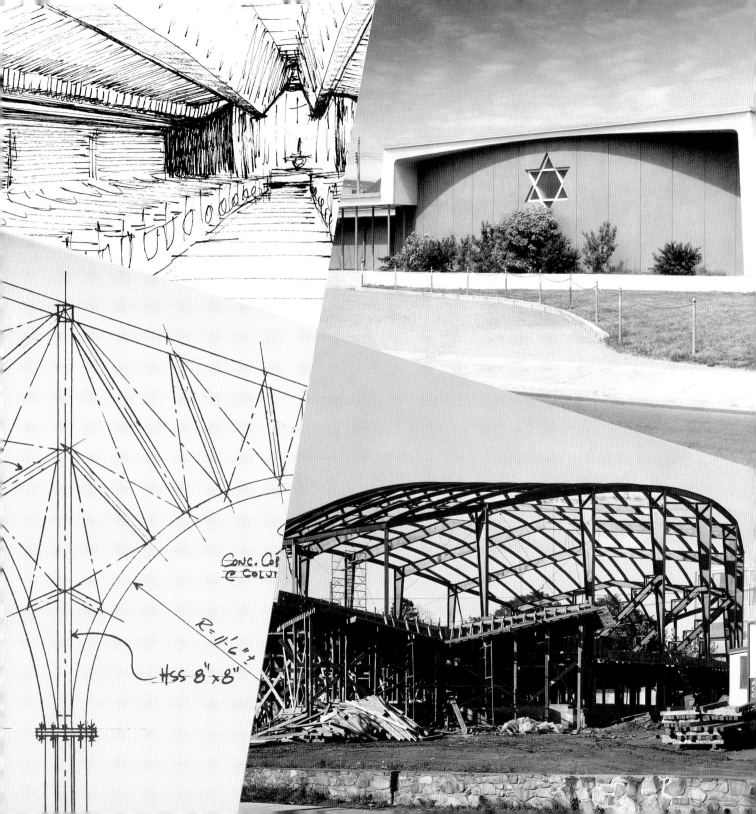

CONC. COL
@ COLUI

R=11'-6"±

HSS 8"x8"

Introduction

Between 1950 and 2000 Atlantic Canadian architects produced a significant body of distinguished work that has had a profound influence on the region's aesthetic, socio-logical, and technological consciousness. Despite this influence, post-war architecture in Atlantic Canada has not been well documented, and many exemplary buildings have been destroyed or altered beyond recognition. The Atlantic Modern project establishes a historical record, while raising public awareness and appreciation of modern architecture in Atlantic Canada. Atlantic Modern consists of exhibits and publications that critically examine regional architecture in a national and international context, creating a record of modern architecture in Atlantic Canada.

1. (clockwise from top left): Holy Redeemer Catholic Church (Alfred Hennessey collection), Beth-El Synagogue (photo: Tootons; Angus Campbell collection), Sexton Memorial Gymnasium (photo: Maurice Crosby; Dalhousie University Archives), Blue Cross Centre (Architects Four Ltd.)

Exhibition

Atlantic Modern: The Architecture of the Atlantic Provinces 1950–2000 was a juried exhibition involving several stages. Through the Atlantic Architects' Initiative, each provincial architectural association was invited to appoint a committee to seek buildings in six categories (commercial, educational, industrial, institutional, residential, and worship), using criteria established by *docomomo international* (international working party for Documentation and Conservation of buildings, sites and neighbourhoods of the Modern Movement). The four committees nominated one project per decade for each building type, totalling 30 projects per province. Only buildings designed by an architectural firm from the Atlantic region were considered.

The full set of nearly 120 nominated buildings was then considered by the exhibition jury. Excellence was the overriding criterion for selection to the exhibition. The jury also sought projects that were exemplary of their time and place of making, and projects that suggested the particular conditions of practice in the Atlantic region.

Research and curatorial work over the next five months included searches of various archives, practice records, publications, and the buildings themselves to verify authorship and dates and to seek original documents. The exhibition presented the harvest of archival material, including photographs, sketches, and architectural drawings, supplemented by photographic reproductions of the original materials and contemporary photographs. It also included a time line of projects and a set of architect's stories, giving a sense of the conditions of architectural practice in the Atlantic region during the Modern period. Specially constructed models gave a taste of the landscape and mass relations, spatial qualities, and material expression of five selected projects.

2. *"Now Open!" advertisement from the* Halifax Mail-Star, *Wednesday, August 22, 1962. Microform. Halifax Regional Library collection.*

Jury Process

The original charge to the provincial committees was to seek out one building from each decade in each of the six building type categories, using the *docomomo* criteria for modern architecture. These criteria were consolidated as follows:

Technical:
- made effective use of new materials
- made effective use of new construction techniques
- established new architectural principles
- served as a model for other buildings or practices

Social:
- was the result of a new social or political strategy
- had a positive impact on the community

Aesthetic:
- exemplified significant formal qualities

Comparative:
- had a significant impact on local practice
- had an impact on national or international practice
- had a technical, functional or formal relation to precedent buildings

A total of 117 nominations were received. The jury's initial review, selecting the best building per type per province, led to a very inconsistent level of quality. Rigid adherence to the intended selection set was abandoned in favour of selecting the best six buildings per province, while aiming for a broad spread of building types and eras. The final set of 26 buildings was the jury's best effort to meet the original objectives of both breadth and excellence in its selections.

The jury was concerned that the relative lack of pre-1985 projects in the New Brunswick nominations led to some imbalance in the overall set of selections. To undertake additional fieldwork in New Brunswick in search of further nominations would have undermined the nomination and jury process and would have led to other imbalances; the jury was resolute in selecting only from the provincial nominations.

At first glance, some nominated projects appeared not to fulfill the criterion of "designed by a regional architectural practice"; respecting the nomination process, the jury did not disqualify projects, but made its selection from all nominated works.

3. Howard House under construction. Photographer: James Steeves, n.d. Brian MacKay-Lyons Architecture and Urban Design collection.

Regional Firms

Uncertainty abounds in authorship, date, proper name, and even the precise location of modern buildings, reflecting the generally sketchy state of awareness and documentation. The oral history is mostly anecdotal, and often biased by misunderstandings, personal agendas, grudges and wishful thinking. For one project, three different but absolutely unshakeable opinions were offered regarding the identity of the design architect.

A few buildings designed by architects "from away" were part of the exhibition, and demonstrated that the work produced in the region stands up well in relation not only to its regional peers, but also nationally. The Dalhousie Thermal Plant was thought at first to have significant regional involvement in the design, but now seems a complete Toronto import. The Marine Sciences Research Laboratory was originally attributed to the Montreal firm Dobush, Stewart & Bourke, but further research suggests that St. John's-based Peter Holtshousen conceived the design in collaboration with the Lab director, Dr. F. A. Aldrich.

Complex geographic relationships exist within projects that were certainly carried out by regional firms. Junji Mikawa, a Japanese architect on a work exchange programme with Fowler Bauld & Mitchell, was a key player in the conceptual and design phases of the Dalhousie Arts Centre, and by some accounts is responsible for the overall form and planning of the building. Jim Donahue, itinerant architect and teacher (at the University of Manitoba) of both Keith Graham and Frank Harrington, was on the design team for the Public Archives of Nova Scotia. He is credited by both of these former students with a crucial role in resolving the detailing strategy of the building and the working relationships within the project team.

Regional Architecture/ Regionalism

The notion of "regional architecture" risks nostalgia and sentimentality, looking only for traces of some imagined, usually traditional, local authenticity within buildings. On the other hand, there is an equal risk of a dismissive and patronizing reading of regionally produced works as derivative, "behind the times" imitations of the important works of the metropolitan avant-garde. In conversation about the works in this exhibition with Dr. Kurt Forster, director of the Canadian Centre for Architecture, he proposed that any critical understanding of regional architecture must work past these easy and generally retrospective traps.

Forster suggested that regional work might be understood better as free from the external pressures of the fashion system and the anxiety of the avant-garde; free to dwell on certain quite fundamental issues that may be passed over in the rush to embrace the newest and latest thing. Regional architects might persist in the study of architectural themes and issues that are not in themselves temporally specific. A critic might see the Canada Permanent Building as derived from the slightly earlier work of the Italian architects Albini and Moretti; is it any less reasonable to suggest that the Canada Permanent Building inspired the 1990s work of the Swiss architects Diener & Diener? Or is it more useful to recognize that the interweaving of the horizontal floor tray with the vertical weft of curtain wall mullions is a persistent theme of modern architecture?

Documentation

The core of the exhibition was the 26 regional buildings selected by the jury. Each building was presented individually with a selection of archival material, including photographs, sketches and architectural drawings. The inclusion of this original material was intended to present the buildings in the context of their design and production, and with respect to the conditions of their time and local situation. The preservation of the records of modern buildings is surprisingly erratic. Sketches and studies, all too rarely preserved, allow an intimate, sometimes indiscreet glimpse of the conception and early development of the design. Photographs and and presentation drawings are much more self-conscious, and portray the project (and the architect) in quite formal terms. Construction and permit drawings are most likely to be preserved, often as prints provided for building permits or as records for building owners. Original working drawings are crucial in establishing the basic facts of the project, but also give a flavour of the care and effort of the designers, and hint at the organization of the architectural practice. For a disappointing number of projects the original drawings are lost, due to the passing of small-scale firms with no successors; more shocking is the policy of a number of larger, ongoing firms to record their legacy of drawings on microfilm and destroy the originals.

Models

Archival material was complemented by architectural models prepared specifically for the exhibition. Most of the buildings are quite distant from the exhibition site, many are not open to the public, and some have been destroyed or altered in significant ways. The models aimed to evoke an enriched sensory experience of these buildings, allowing a spatial appreciation of the documentary material on the walls. The 1:50 scale models of the Beth-El Synagogue and Belvedere Golf and Winter Club portrayed each building in relation to its landscape and local context. 1:20 scale models of the ceiling spaces of Newfoundland House and Holy Redeemer Church invoked a bodily sense of the spatial and geometric experience of these buildings. The original curtain wall of the Canada Permanent Building was reconstructed at half-size, providing a taste of the subtle visual experience (now lost) of its original state.

4. Entry, Lobby and Sculpture Gallery, design presentation drawing from brochure "the arts centre," Dalhousie University, Halifax, NS, n.d. [1967]. Offset print on paper. Junji Mikawa collection.

Outrages, Tragedies and Risks

Modern buildings are almost entirely without protection, and are vulnerable to destruction and insensitive alteration. Most often (as in the current situation at Beth-El Synagogue) the public and the architectural community are unaware of the danger until the damage has begun. Public awareness, documentation, and legislation are all required to ensure that our modern legacy is sustained for future generations. The current roster of destroyed, altered and threatened buildings is lengthy:

The PEI Ark: Destroyed mid-2000.

Beth-El Synagogue: Glazed "Star of David" lattice wall at main space removed ca. 1998. Portico destroyed, entry doors relocated to curved wall, and main room subdivided in early 2001. Library and office wing destroyed 2002.

Forest Road Nonprofit Housing: Window replacement in 2001 removed oversized head and sill trim. Repainted in 2002 using earth tones instead of bright original colours.

5. Photo of demolition in progress, Beth-El Synagogue, St. John's, NL, April 2001. Photographer: Chad Jamieson.

Newfoundland House: Not maintained by the province between 1963 and 1990, when ownership was returned to the Smallwood family. Poorly maintained since then, with many improvised repairs (screen doors, plywood lean-to shelters, etc.), severe water leakage and deterioration of exterior and interior materials.

Canada Permanent Building: The light porcelain enamel panels were painted black in the late 1990s, and the window washing rail removed, spoiling much of the transparency of the curtain wall. The stairs at Barrington Street were also removed, and the interconnected space between mezzanine and ground floor closed in.

Marine Sciences Research Laboratory: Phylarium tank removed, glazed roof replaced with shingles, and space subdivided for new offices in early 2001.

Dalhousie Arts Centre: Chronic deferred maintenance for several decades has led to major deterioration of the exterior surfaces and interior finishes.

St. Bride's College: The college moved to the Memorial University campus in the late 1960s. The dormitory wing is used for conferences and retreats. The classroom wing was converted into a Catholic school, which closed in the late 1990s. No new use has been identified.

In addition to the threats to buildings, many of the documents and records of modern architecture have been lost. Many firms destroyed their original drawings after making microfilm records, while others simply disposed of their records. A clear policy for preserving these records must be promoted by the provincial architectural associations, and appropriate archives must be identified.

The Atlantic Modern Project

The Atlantic Modern Project is an ongoing effort to build a documentary history of modern architecture in Atlantic Canada. The total project included the exhibition, an exhibition catalogue, and a web-based gallery and database. Continuing research work includes fieldwork to identify exemplary modern buildings; interviews of Atlantic architects to fill out the oral history of regional practice; and identification of archival sources.

Web Site

The Gallery of Modern Architecture in Atlantic Canada is a searchable database of images and information about the buildings in the exhibition and others in the Atlantic region. It is curated by Donna Richardson and Helen Powell, and is available on the World Wide Web: http://www2.lib.unb.ca/AtlanticArchitecture.

Opportunities

The Gallery of Modern Architecture in Atlantic Canada will be expanded regularly. We encourage nominations of worthy modern buildings from all parts of the Atlantic provinces for the expanded Gallery and for future research, exhibition and publication. We are also interested in the story of modern architecture in the region, and we welcome submissions from architects, builders, clients, users and observers. Submit nominations and stories to Atlantic Modern, c/o Faculty of Architecture and Planning, Dalhousie University, P.O. Box 1000 Central Station, Halifax, Nova Scotia B3J 2X4.

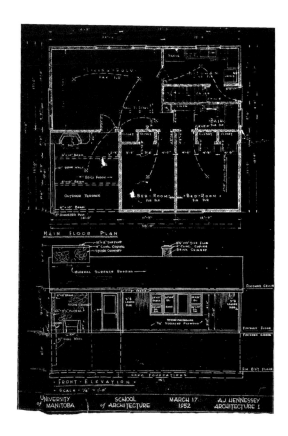

6. "House design for Architecture 1, University of Manitoba School of Architecture" plan and elevation design drawing, March 17, 1952. Delineator: Alfred Hennessey. Blueprint. Alfred Hennessey collection.
7. (page 10) Detail of model of curtain wall of Canada Permanent Building, Halifax, NS. Modelmakers: Ania Gudelewicz, Melanie Hayne, Darren Newton, Jennifer Uegama. Photographer: Ken Kam.

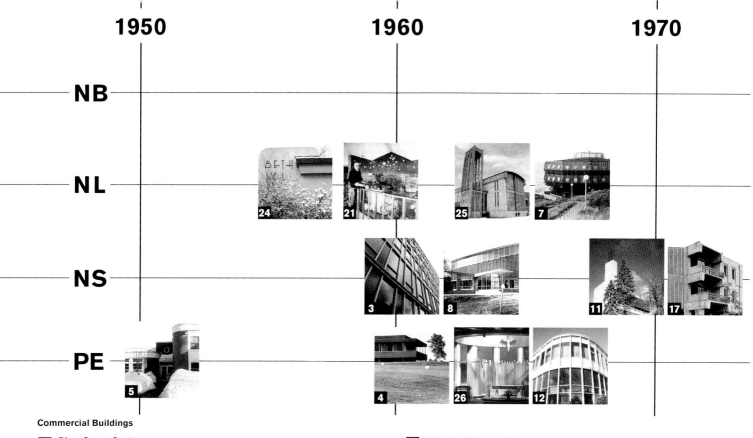

	1950		1960		1970
NB					
NL			24 21 25 7		
NS			3 8		11 17
PE	5		4 26 12		

Commercial Buildings

1 **Blue Cross Centre**
644 Main Street, Moncton, NB — 1987–1988
Architectural firm: ARCOP Architects
Architectural firm: Architects Four Ltd.
Principal architect: Robert Eaton
Design architects: Pierre Gallant, Paul Hughes, Andrew McGillivary

2 **Marble Mountain Ski Lodge**
Marble Mountain, Corner Brook, NL — 1992–1996
Architectural firm: Byrne Architects Inc.
Design architects: Michael Byrne, Gregor Byrne

3 **Canada Permanent Building**
1646 Barrington Street, Halifax, NS — 1961–1962
Architectural firm: C.A. Fowler & Company, Engineers & Architects
Design architects: Charles A. Fowler, Jamie MacDonald

4 **Belvedere Golf and Winter Club, Clubhouse**
1 Greensview Drive, Charlottetown, PE — 1962–1963
Architectural firm: Alfred J. Hennessey Architect
Design architect: Alfred Hennessey

5 **Polyclinic**
178 Fitzroy Street, Charlottetown, PE — 1945–1949
Architectural firm: E. S. Blanchard Architect
Design architects: E. Stirling Blanchard, James F. Toombs

Educational Buildings

6 **La Dune de Bouctouche: Irving Eco-Centre**
Bouctouche, NB — 1996–1997
Architectural firm: Architects Four Ltd. / Elide Albert Architect Ltd.
Principal architect: Elide Albert
Design architect: Andrew McGillivary

7 **Marine Sciences Research Laboratory**
Logy Bay, NL — 1964–1967
Architectural firm: Dobush, Stewart, Bourke, Holtshousen
Design architect: Peter Holtshousen
Executive architect: Sir Christopher Barlow

8 **Sexton Memorial Gymnasium, Nova Scotia Technical College**
1360 Barrington Street, Halifax, NS — 1960–1963
Architectural firm: Duffus Romans & Single, Architects & Engineers
Architect: Andris Kundzins

9 **Charlottetown Rural High School**
100 Burns Crescent, Charlottetown, PE — 1992–1994
Architectural firm: Bergmark & Hammarlund Architects
Design architect: David Bergmark

Industrial Buildings

10 **Hibernia Topside Facilities: Living quarters and service module**
Bull Arm, NL — 1990–1995
Architectural firm: Newfoundland Offshore Contractors
Architectural firm: BFL Consultants Ltd.
Design architect: Jim Case

11 **Dalhousie University Thermal Plant**
1236 Henry Street, Halifax, NS — 1969–1970
Architectural firm: Hancock, Little, Calvert & Associates
Design architect: L. S. Langmead

12 **Central Creameries, New Production Plant**
215 Fitzroy Street, Charlottetown, PE — 1966–1967
Architectural firm: Keith Pickard Architect
Design architect: Keith Pickard

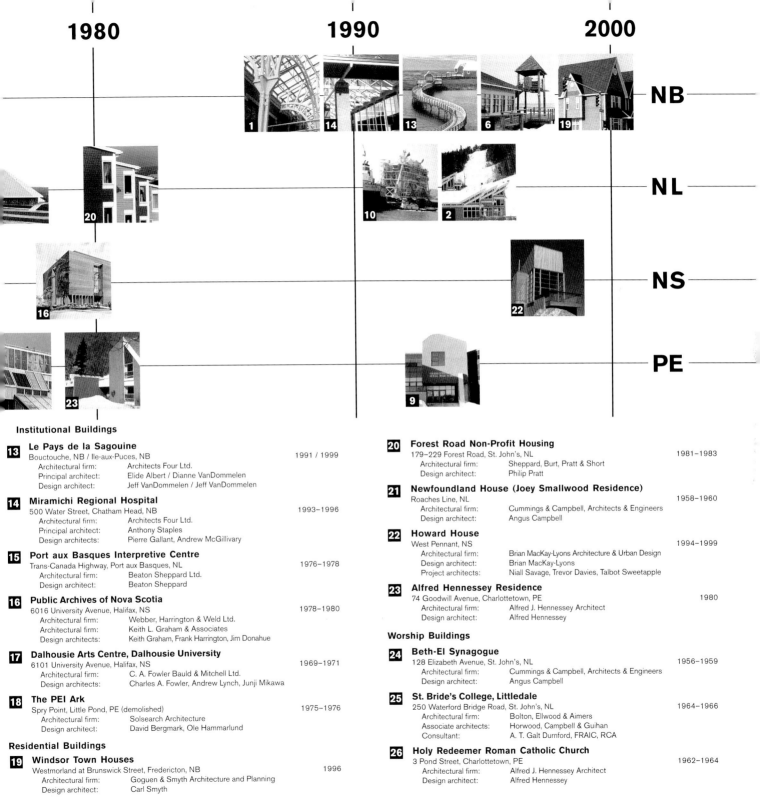

1980　　　**1990**　　　**2000**

NB

NL

NS

PE

Institutional Buildings

13 **Le Pays de la Sagouine**
Bouctouche, NB / Ile-aux-Puces, NB
Architectural firm: Architects Four Ltd.
Principal architect: Elide Albert / Dianne VanDommelen
Design architect: Jeff VanDommelen / Jeff VanDommelen
1991 / 1999

14 **Miramichi Regional Hospital**
500 Water Street, Chatham Head, NB
Architectural firm: Architects Four Ltd.
Principal architect: Anthony Staples
Design architects: Pierre Gallant, Andrew McGillivary
1993–1996

15 **Port aux Basques Interpretive Centre**
Trans-Canada Highway, Port aux Basques, NL
Architectural firm: Beaton Sheppard Ltd.
Design architect: Beaton Sheppard
1976–1978

16 **Public Archives of Nova Scotia**
6016 University Avenue, Halifax, NS
Architectural firm: Webber, Harrington & Weld Ltd.
Architectural firm: Keith L. Graham & Associates
Design architects: Keith Graham, Frank Harrington, Jim Donahue
1978–1980

17 **Dalhousie Arts Centre, Dalhousie University**
6101 University Avenue, Halifax, NS
Architectural firm: C. A. Fowler Bauld & Mitchell Ltd.
Design architects: Charles A. Fowler, Andrew Lynch, Junji Mikawa
1969–1971

18 **The PEI Ark**
Spry Point, Little Pond, PE (demolished)
Architectural firm: Solsearch Architecture
Design architect: David Bergmark, Ole Hammarlund
1975–1976

Residential Buildings

19 **Windsor Town Houses**
Westmorland at Brunswick Street, Fredericton, NB
Architectural firm: Goguen & Smyth Architecture and Planning
Design architect: Carl Smyth
1996

20 **Forest Road Non-Profit Housing**
179–229 Forest Road, St. John's, NL
Architectural firm: Sheppard, Burt, Pratt & Short
Design architect: Philip Pratt
1981–1983

21 **Newfoundland House (Joey Smallwood Residence)**
Roaches Line, NL
Architectural firm: Cummings & Campbell, Architects & Engineers
Design architect: Angus Campbell
1958–1960

22 **Howard House**
West Pennant, NS
Architectural firm: Brian MacKay-Lyons Architecture & Urban Design
Design architect: Brian MacKay-Lyons
Project architects: Niall Savage, Trevor Davies, Talbot Sweetapple
1994–1999

23 **Alfred Hennessey Residence**
74 Goodwill Avenue, Charlottetown, PE
Architectural firm: Alfred J. Hennessey Architect
Design architect: Alfred Hennessey
1980

Worship Buildings

24 **Beth-El Synagogue**
128 Elizabeth Avenue, St. John's, NL
Architectural firm: Cummings & Campbell, Architects & Engineers
Design architect: Angus Campbell
1956–1959

25 **St. Bride's College, Littledale**
250 Waterford Bridge Road, St. John's, NL
Architectural firm: Bolton, Ellwood & Aimers
Associate architects: Horwood, Campbell & Guihan
Consultant: A. T. Galt Durnford, FRAIC, RCA
1964–1966

26 **Holy Redeemer Roman Catholic Church**
3 Pond Street, Charlottetown, PE
Architectural firm: Alfred J. Hennessey Architect
Design architect: Alfred Hennessey
1962–1964

Nova Scotia

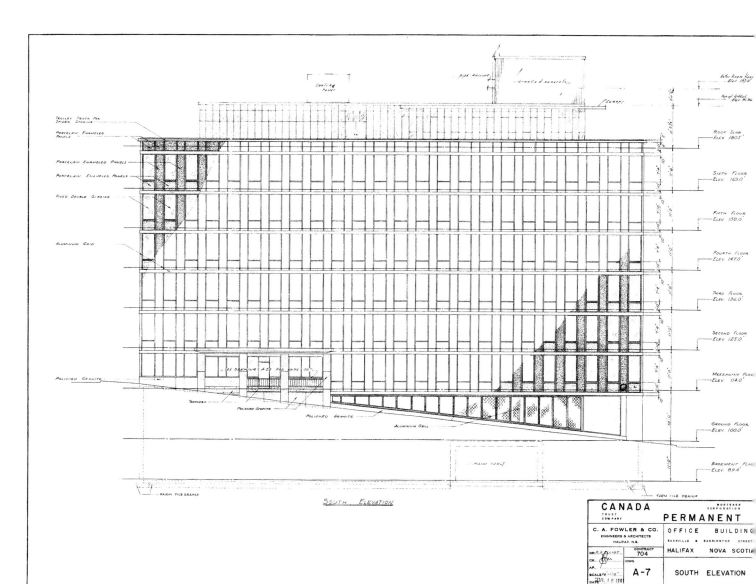

TROLLEY TRACK FOR SPIDER STAGING

PORCELAIN ENAMELED PANELS

PORCELAIN ENAMELED PANELS

PORCELAIN ENAMELED PANELS

FIXED DOUBLE GLAZING

ALUMINUM GRID

POLISHED GRANITE

SEE DRAWING A-21 FOR DETAIL OF

TERRAZZO

POLISHED GRANITE

POLISHED GRANITE

ALUMINUM GRILL

FARM TILE DRAINS

FARM TILE DRAINS

Cooling Tower

Pipe Railing

Grooved connection

Canopy

Water Room Floor
Elev. 191.0'

Top of Ladder
Elev. 191.66'

ROOF SLAB
ELEV. 180.5'

SIXTH FLOOR
ELEV. 169.0'

FIFTH FLOOR
ELEV. 158.0'

FOURTH FLOOR
ELEV. 147.0'

THIRD FLOOR
ELEV. 136.0'

SECOND FLOOR
ELEV. 125.0'

MEZZANINE FLOOR
ELEV. 114.0'

GROUND FLOOR
ELEV. 100.0'

BASEMENT FLOOR
ELEV. 89.0'

MAIN VAULT

SOUTH ELEVATION

| CANADA | MORTGAGE CORPORATION |
| TRUST COMPANY | PERMANENT |

C. A. FOWLER & CO.	OFFICE BUILDING
ENGINEERS & ARCHITECTS	
HALIFAX, N.S.	SACKVILLE & BARRINGTON STREET

DR. R.G. ELLIOT	CONTRACT 704	HALIFAX NOVA SCOTIA
CK.	DWG.	
AF.	A-7	SOUTH ELEVATION
SCALE 1/8"=1'0"		
DATE JUL 15 1981		

Canada Permanent Building

1961–1962
1646 Barrington Street, Halifax, NS
Architectural firm: C.A. Fowler & Company, Engineers & Architects, Halifax, NS
Design architects: Charles A. Fowler, Jamie MacDonald

A Tower of Glass and Steel ... The City's First Completed Curtain Wall Structure ... 7000 Square Feet of Glass, 2 Miles of Wire, 2000 Tons of Structural Steel ...

- Halifax Chronicle-Herald

The new headquarters for Canada Permanent Trust was celebrated as the very image of progress, and a sign of the imminent arrival of the future in Halifax. Even during construction, its steel frame was featured in news photos describing it as an "ultra modern structure." C.A. Fowler's office had previously completed a number of projects for the Trust when a fire burned its Halifax headquarters. The Trust came to Fowler, asking for a very traditional three-storey masonry building. Their inability to purchase the lot to the north left them with a very long, thin end block site ill-suited to a mass building, and Fowler convinced them that seven stories of lightweight, steel and curtain wall construction would create much more workable spaces. Contemporary legal reforms had allowed the trusts to become more like banks in their operations, and the transparency achieved in the building would become a key element of the Trust's new progressive image.

A staccato rhythm of vertical aluminum mullions plays against concave bands at the upper floor lines, with light and dark grey enamel infill panels playing against the glass to create a sense of layered transparency. This curtain wall lattice runs along Barrington Street, stretches up Sackville Street and then back on Argyle Street to meet the party wall to the north, making no distinction between front, side and rear, and creating a unique "end cap" to the block. Built tight to the street lines, the prism of the upper floors reinforces the traditional urban block structure of the city. These office floors are simply organized, a large loft of open office space with a single internal row of columns to screen the service zone along the party wall. At the Barrington end, the obtuse angles of the elevator core set up a diamond theme that extends to paving, flooring and drop ceiling patterns. The slope of the site is used to create ground-level entrances at two levels, from Barrington into the banking hall and from Sackville into the trust offices. A sculpted terrazzo stair connecting the public floors occupied much of the Barrington Street display window, while a pentagonal atrium joined these spaces within.

8. *"South Elevation" contract drawing #704-A2, July 15, 1961. Delineator: R. G. Elliot. Pencil and ink on vellum. Fowler Bauld & Mitchell Ltd. collection.*
9. *View from southeast, May 2001. Photographer: Chad Jamieson.*

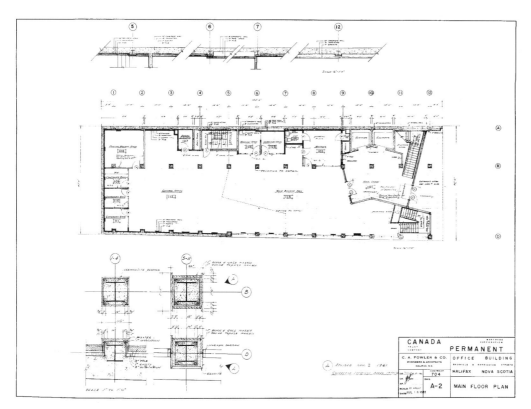

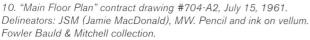

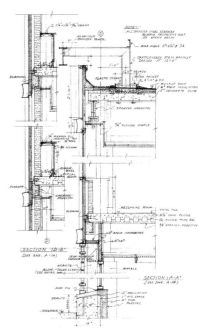

10. "Main Floor Plan" contract drawing #704-A2, July 15, 1961.
Delineators: JSM (Jamie MacDonald), MW. Pencil and ink on vellum.
Fowler Bauld & Mitchell collection.
11. Detail of "Upper Wall Sections" contract drawing #704-S9, July 15,
1961. Delineator: CAF (Charles A. Fowler). Ink and pencil on sepia print.
Fowler Bauld & Mitchell collection.
12. "Detail - South Wall Grillwork" contract drawing #704-A22, July 15,
1961. Delineator: HK. Pencil and ink on vellum. Fowler Bauld & Mitchell
collection.

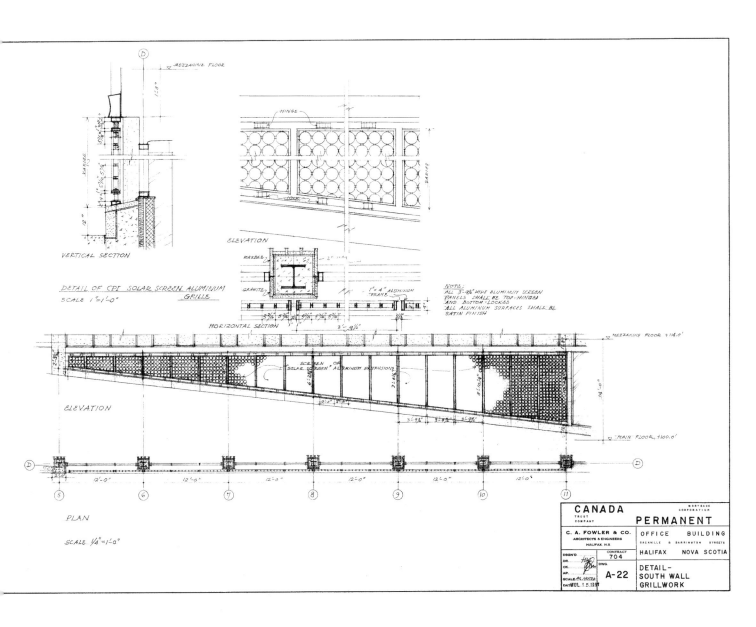

MEZZANINE FLOOR

HINGE

VERTICAL SECTION

DETAIL OF CPI SOLAR SCREEN ALUMINUM
GRILLE

SCALE 1"=1'-0"

ELEVATION

MARBLE

GRANITE

1"x 4" ALUMINUM
FRAME

HORIZONTAL SECTION

3'-9½"

NOTE:
ALL 3'-9½" WIDE ALUMINUM SCREEN
PANELS SHALL BE TOP-HINGED
AND BOTTOM-LOCKED
ALL ALUMINUM SURFACES SHALL BE
SATIN FINISH

MEZZANINE FLOOR +114.0'

SCREEN OR
"SOLAR SCREEN" ALUMINUM EXTRUSIONS

ELEVATION

MAIN FLOOR +100.0'

PLAN

SCALE ¼"=1'-0"

D   5   6   7   8   9   10   11   D
      12'-0"   12'-0"   12'-0"   12'-0"   12'-0"   12'-0"

CANADA
TRUST
COMPANY

MORTGAGE
CORPORATION

PERMANENT

C. A. FOWLER & CO.
ARCHITECTS & ENGINEERS
HALIFAX, N.S

OFFICE   BUILDING
SACKVILLE & BARRINGTON STREETS

HALIFAX   NOVA SCOTIA

DSGN'D
DR.
CK.
AP.
SCALE AS NOTED
DATE JUL. 15 195?

CONTRACT
704

DWG.
A-22

DETAIL -
SOUTH WALL
GRILLWORK

Sexton Memorial Gymnasium

1960–1963 Nova Scotia Technical College
1360 Barrington Street, Halifax, NS
Architectural firm: Duffus Romans & Single, Architects & Engineers, Halifax, NS
Architect: Andris Kundzins

A major alumni fundraising effort resulted in the building of the gymnasium, a memorial to Tech founder F. H. Sexton. This was the second major element in the early 1960s modernization of the Tech campus, following upon the floating concrete frame and highly glazed curtain wall of the new administration and classroom building. Early studies for the gymnasium considered more conservative expressions, including a repetitive barrel shell roof over a rectangular plan, but the alumni building committee were strong supporters of the elliptical plan with sloped curving roof. The project files contain studies of this expressive form in alternate locations, most provocatively at the corner of Spring Garden Road and Queen Street.

Sexton Gymnasium's play of three-dimensional curves has some kinship with a number of exuberant contemporary campus athletic buildings, in particular Saarinen's Yale hockey rink. Andris Kundzins's design for Tech stands apart in its melding of highly expressive form with very straightforward means of construction. Where Saarinen's forms are realized using complex and expensive concrete arch and cable net construction, the Sexton Gymnasium uses a series of simple steel portal frames to span the width, each shifting in width and height like the station molds of a boat's hull, while straight lines of joists and steel deck are aligned to develop the compound ruled surfaces of the roof. Deeply ribbed brick cladding appears to float above the glazed base, while a continuous translucent clerestory lifts the roof above the corrugated brick. The angled butterfly roof of the glass vestibule provides a razor-sharp

accent to the floating curves of the main volume. The 1963 Canadian Steel Conference acclaimed the Sexton Gymnasium as Canada's most beautiful steel building of the year.

Project designer Andris Kundzins would later become a partner in the Duffus firm. The Sexton Gymnasium files contain a wealth of perspective studies initialled "P. K." for Paul Kundzins, Andris's father and a renowned architect in his native Latvia. Paul's brother Harald Kundzins worked in C.A. Fowler's office and was one of the draughtsmen on the Canada Permanent project.

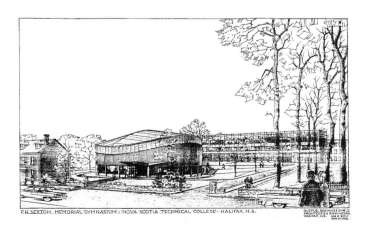

13. View from Barrington Street upon completion, n.d. Dalhousie University Archive collection.
14. "F.H. Sexton Memorial Gymnasium" perspective view from Barrington Street, presentation drawing, January 5, 1962. Delineator: PK (Paul Kundzins). Microform. Duffus Romans Kundzins Rounsefell Ltd. collection.

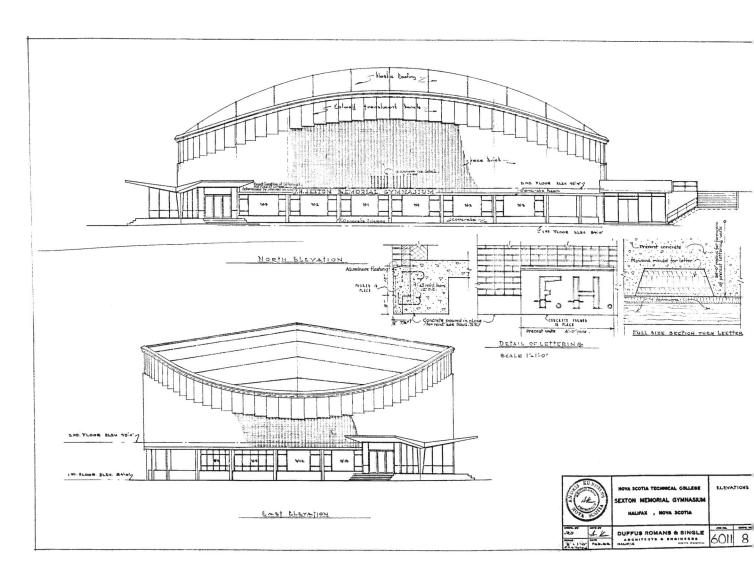

NORTH ELEVATION

DETAIL OF LETTERING

SCALE 1"=1'-0"

FULL SIZE SECTION THRU LETTER

EAST ELEVATION

NOVA SCOTIA TECHNICAL COLLEGE	ELEVATIONS
SEXTON MEMORIAL GYMNASIUM	
HALIFAX , NOVA SCOTIA	
DUFFUS ROMANS & SINGLE	JOB NO. 6011	DWG. NO. 8
ARCHITECTS & ENGINEERS HALIFAX NOVA SCOTIA	

15. *"Elevations" contract drawing #6011-8, February 1962. Delineator: JRD. Microform. Duffus Romans Kundzins Rounsefell Ltd. collection.*

18

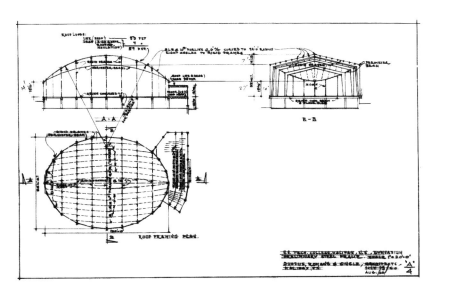

16. "Preliminary Steel Frame" contract drawing #"A"-4, July 19, 1960. No delineator. Microform. Duffus Romans Kundzins Rounsefell Ltd. collection.
17. Detail of exterior wall surface, May 2001. Photographer: Chad Jamieson.
18. View of steel framing, n.d. Photographer: Maurice Crosby. Dalhousie University Archive collection.

Dalhousie University Thermal Plant

1969–1970 Dalhousie University
1236 Henry Street, Halifax, NS
Architectural firm: Hancock, Little, Calvert & Associates, Toronto, ON
Design architect: L. S. Langmead

The new central thermal plant forms part of Dalhousie's very ambitious building activities of the late 1960s and early 1970s. The lead consultant was the mechanical engineering firm Crossey Associates. Oral tradition suggested that university architect Jim Sykes, formerly of John Andrews's office in Toronto, had a key role in the design. Sykes disclaims authorship, and the drawings suggest that L. S. Langmead, later a partner in Hancock Little Calvert, was the design architect. The bold massing and extensive use of exposed concrete in the thermal plant reflects the influence of John Andrews's Scarborough College project and the contemporary fascination with megastructures in Canadian practice. The same spirit is carried forward in the Dalhousie Arts Centre, the Life Sciences complex, the Killam Library and the system of lower-level connecting links and classrooms installed beneath Dalhousie's 1920s stone campus, all of which suggest that Sykes was very much the godfather-architect of the campus expansion.

The twin towers of concrete are stepped and sculpted to create a bold skyward thrust, and support between them a metal-clad bridge volume containing offices for the university's facilities managers. From any distance the building evokes strong associations with the work of the Italian Futurist architects of the 1910s, especially the fantastic perspective drawings of Antonio Saint'Elia. Up close, this large-scale sculpted building mass reveals itself to be, paradoxically, quite well behaved in relation to the neighbouring houses.

19. "Dalhousie University Thermal Plant" perspective view from southeast, presentation drawing #1, November 11, 1969. Diazoprint. Dalhousie University Facilities Management collection.
20. View from southwest, May 2001. Photographer: Chad Jamieson.

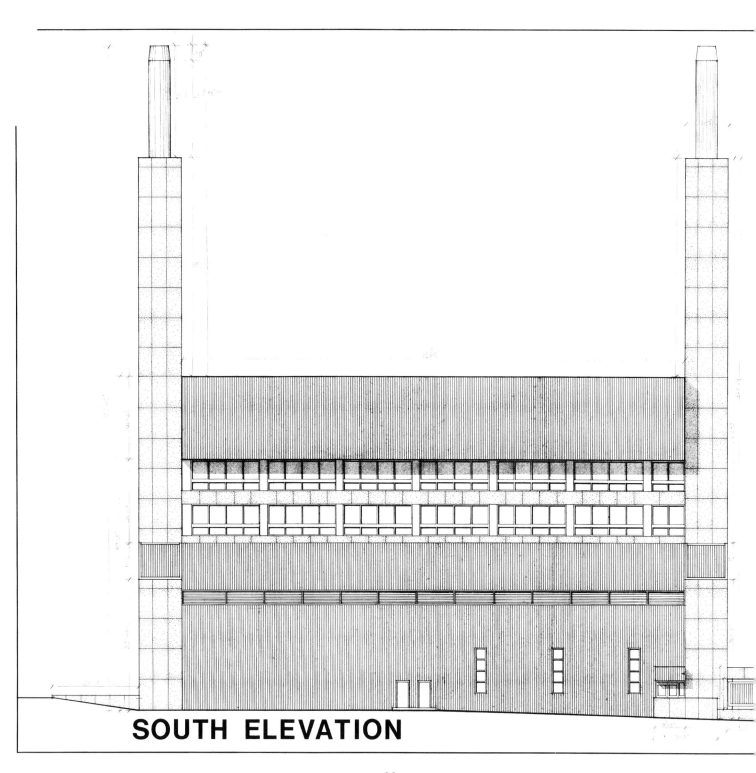

SOUTH ELEVATION

Revisions

Date	Description

Approval

DALHOUSIE UNIVERSITY
THERMAL PLANT

**Hancock
Little
Calvert
Associates**

Consultants in Town Planning,
Architecture,
Landscape Architecture
and Municipal Engineering

40 Irwin Avenue
Toronto 5, Canada
Telephone (416) 925-1411

SOUTH ELEVATION

Drawing No.	Job File	·	25-2-2
3	Drawn	·	K.G. VILLIERS
	Checked	·	L.S. LANGMEAD
	Date	·	NOV. 10 1969
	Scale	·	1/8" = 1'-0"

*21. "South Elevation" presentation drawing #2512-2 no.3,
November 10, 1969. Delineator: K. G. Villiers. Diazoprint with
pencil additions. Dalhousie University Facilities Management
collection.
22. View from southeast, May 2001. Photographer: Chad Jamieson.*

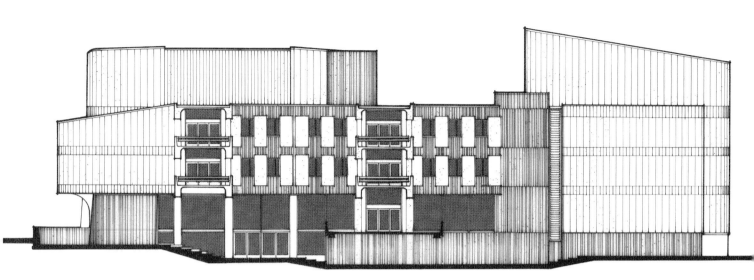

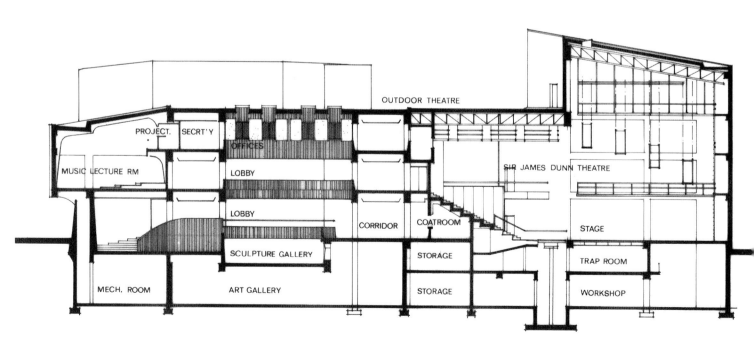

OUTDOOR THEATRE

PROJECT. | SECRT'Y

OFFICES

MUSIC LECTURE RM

LOBBY

SIR JAMES DUNN THEATRE

LOBBY

CORRIDOR | COATROOM

STAGE

SCULPTURE GALLERY

STORAGE

MECH. ROOM | ART GALLERY

STORAGE

TRAP ROOM

WORKSHOP

Dalhousie Arts Centre

1969–1971 Dalhousie University
6101 University Avenue, Halifax, NS
Architectural firm: C. A. Fowler Bauld & Mitchell Ltd., Halifax, NS
Design architects: Charles A. Fowler, Andrew Lynch, Junji Mikawa

By far the most radical of the new Dalhousie campus buildings of the late 1960s, the Arts Centre is a phantasmagorical composition, part giant-scale insect carapace, part fragment of an imaginary Japanese metabolist cityscape. Along University Avenue the building takes its place in the parade of "big facades," undermining the stuffy proprieties of neighbouring buildings while conforming to the general typology of a formal frontage. Stub concrete bridges are combined with hollows and wells at grade and a play of recess and projection in the dark concrete surfaces, creating a rich facade animated by the fact and potential of human inhabitation. The stub bridges were meant merely to suggest the potential of connections across University Avenue, while actual bridges were proposed over the side streets to connect to future neighbours. An elevated terrace at the rear begins an exterior route up to the secret theatre space of the roof terrace, a space which now lies dormant, awaiting an imaginative proposal from the Dalhousie community.

The obsessive connection-making of the exterior carries forward in the main lobby, a wonderfully fluid multi-storey landscape of stairs and balconies rendered in concrete and glass. The various contingent fragments of lobby space serve each particular component of the Centre, but can also be brought together around the tall atrium to form a very fine space for choral performance. In contrast to the lobby, the two theatre spaces and the art gallery are quite self-contained and self-absorbed spaces.

A variety of hands is apparent in the design at the level of detail and finishes. Junji Mikawa, a Japanese architect working in C. A. Fowler's office on a work exchange programme, would seem to be the author of the massing and organization of the building, and the driving force behind the metabolist-inspired connecting bridges, castellated concrete girders and blunt detailing of the public spaces. Andrew Lynch took over the project after Mikawa returned to Japan, when the working drawings were complete but the interior finishes were not fully resolved. In contrast to the exterior, the interior of the Rebecca Cohn Auditorium was given a very fine-grained expression of wood battens and curved plaster soffits, clearly inspired by the work of Alvar Aalto.

23. "South Elevation" presentation drawing, n.d. Ink on mylar. Fowler Bauld & Mitchell collection.
24. "Section" presentation drawing, n.d. Ink on mylar. Fowler Bauld & Mitchell collection.
25. Interior of the Rebecca Cohn Auditorium, looking towards the stage, n.d. Fowler Bauld & Mitchell collection.

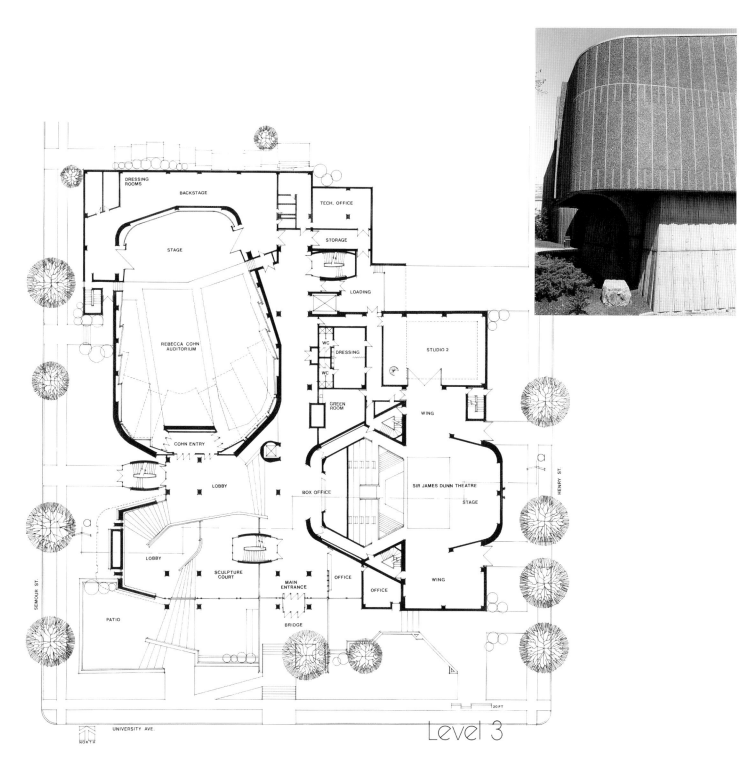

DRESSING
ROOMS

BACKSTAGE

TECH. OFFICE

STAGE

STORAGE

LOADING

REBECCA COHN
AUDITORIUM

WC

DRESSING

STUDIO 2

WC

COHN ENTRY

GREEN
ROOM

WING

LOBBY

BOX OFFICE

SIR JAMES DUNN THEATRE

STAGE

HENRY ST.

LOBBY

SCULPTURE
COURT

OFFICE

WING

MAIN
ENTRANCE

OFFICE

SEMOUR ST.

PATIO

BRIDGE

20 FT

UNIVERSITY AVE.

NORTH

Level 3

26

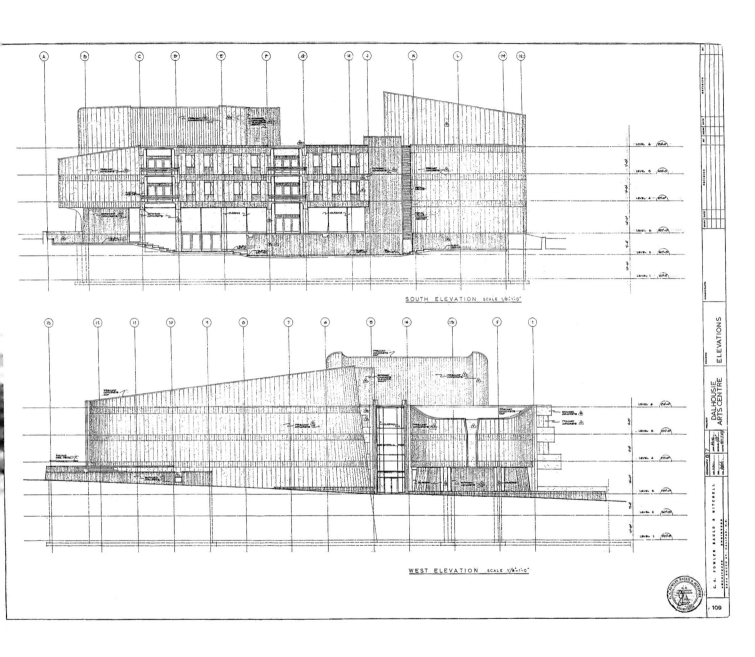

SOUTH ELEVATION SCALE 1/8"=1'-0"

WEST ELEVATION SCALE 1/8"=1'-0"

26. *Detail of precast cladding at rounded corner, May 2001. Photographer: Chad Jamieson.*
27. *"Level 3" plan, presentation drawing, n.d. Ink and tone on mylar. Fowler Bauld & Mitchell collection.*
28. *"Elevations" contract drawing #817-109, March 7, 1969. Delineators: JM (Junji Mikawa), RJC. Microform. Fowler Bauld & Mitchell collection.*

Public Archives of Nova Scotia

1978–1980
6016 University Avenue, Halifax, NS
Architectural firm: Webber, Harrington & Weld Ltd., Halifax, NS
Architectural firm: Keith L. Graham & Associates, Halifax, NS
Design architects: Keith Graham, Frank Harrington, Jim Donahue

The resolute brick mass of the Public Archives of Nova Scotia gives public expression to its role as the provincial treasure house. The vault-like image is sustained by the absence of punched openings in the upper brick walls, and underscored by the deeply recessed windows at the base. Deep multi-storey cuts in plan at the centre of each facade emphasize the building's prismatic mass, and shelter glazed walls to light the circulation and work areas. Closer examination of the apparently unrelieved brick surfaces reveals a subtle use of brickwork traditions – rowlock coursing at the floor levels, brick sills and jack arches – to enliven the otherwise uncompromising sculptural form. Within, a similar relentless material expression prevails, with the use of exposed concrete waffle-slab ceilings and round concrete columns throughout. Detail again provides the relief, in a carefully resolved system of concrete block walls, wood-framed glazed partitions and doors, and wood trim.

Keith Graham Associates received the commission from the Board of the Archives, and the conceptual design (by Graham, Jim Donahue and Michael Byrne) was complete when the province insisted on a shotgun marriage with Webber Harrington & Weld. What might have been a very fractious design development process was rescued by the presence of Donahue, who had taught both Keith Graham and Frank Harrington at the University of Manitoba. According to both architects, Donahue's role in the project was crucial, both in the project process and in the design work.

You don't know how much time we spent on the round columns and how we were going to get the services down in them, and how a block partition should meet a round column. That was a Jim Donahue problem. He would agonize over how he would make that junction of a square block and a round column.

- Frank Harrington

29. Perspective rendering, n.d. WHW collection.
30. Brick detailing at lower level windows, May 2001. Photographer: Chad Jamieson.

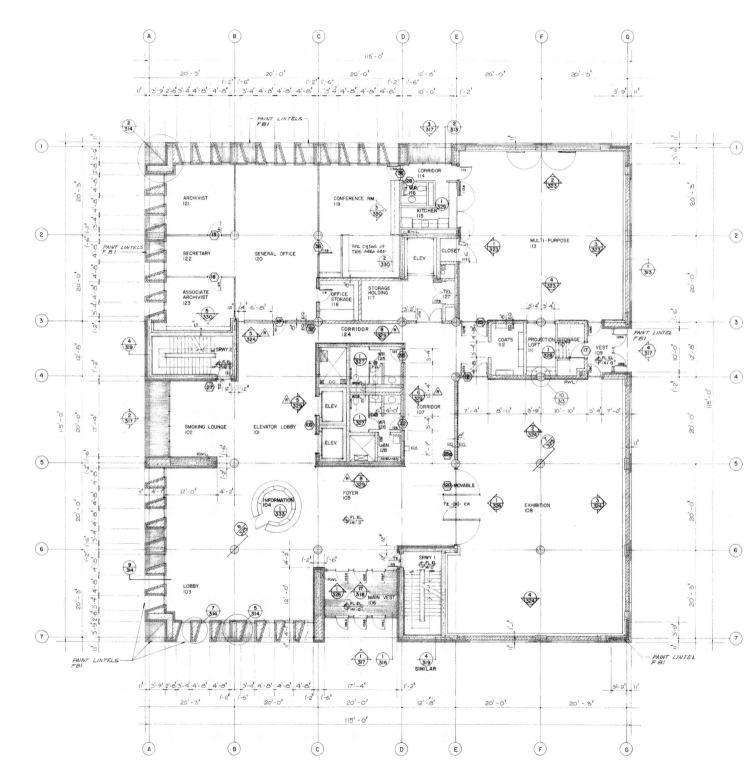

30

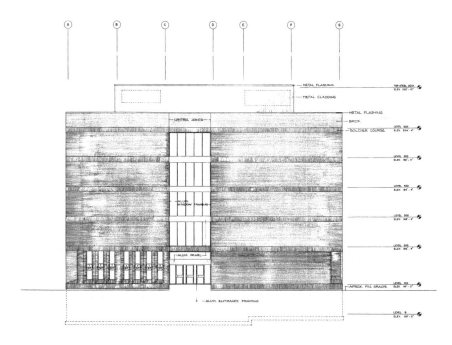

31. *"Level 100 Floor Plan" contract drawing #302.7, June 15, 1979. Delineator: NF. Pencil and ink on vellum. WHW collection.*
32. *Corner detail, May 2001. Photographer: Chad Jamieson.*
33. *View from northeast, n.d. WHW collection.*
34. *"North Elevation" contract drawing #309.1, July 4, 1978. Delineator: NF. Pencil and ink on vellum. WHW collection.*

Howard House

1994–1999
West Pennant, NS
Architectural firm: Brian MacKay-Lyons Architecture Urban Design, Halifax, NS
Design architect: Brian MacKay-Lyons
Project architects: Niall Savage, Trevor Davies, Talbot Sweetapple

The Howard House forms part of the architect's "Houses on the Nova Scotia Coast," a self-conscious set of explorations into the role of constructional and climatic vernaculars in the development of architectural language. Coastal conditions are extreme, and extremely changeable. The air is laden with salt, the soil is thin and rocky, and a typical winter's day will see multiple freeze-thaw cycles, all of which constitute a direct assault on the fabric of buildings. Winds are often heavy, and the rain tends to drive horizontally more often than it falls downwards. In coastal situations wind loads are often much more significant to the building structure than gravity.

The Howard House reflects MacKay-Lyons's characteristic approach to these conditions, with a mixture of bravado and careful preparation. The house sits on an exposed promontory and presents itself as a hugely attenuated, tall and thin volume, almost a sail in the face of the ocean winds. This volume is pierced halfway along by a court that also serves to relieve the wind loads, and is buttressed by a massive concrete stair volume near the shore end. Metal cladding provides an insulated weatherproof overcoat, floating free of the structural frame and the interior partitions. This metal wrapper follows the innate, unself-conscious order of the material and its assembly process, representing the economy of its own making. The interior is organized by a series of larger and smaller spatial bays, arrayed to form a tartan plan grid of ceremonial and service spaces.

More and more, the work is about the landscape and the weather, and the implications of these as form givers, as sources for detail and construction. In the Maritimes, it is always windy.

- Brian MacKay-Lyons

35. View from across the cove. Photographer: James Steeves, n.d. Brian MacKay-Lyons Architecture & Urban Design collection.
36. View of oceanfront window. Photographer: James Steeves, n.d. Brian MacKay-Lyons Architecture & Urban Design collection.
37. (overleaf) Plan with projected section and elevation, presentation drawing, n.d. Delineator: Trevor Davies. Ink on mylar. Brian MacKay-Lyons Architecture & Urban Design collection.

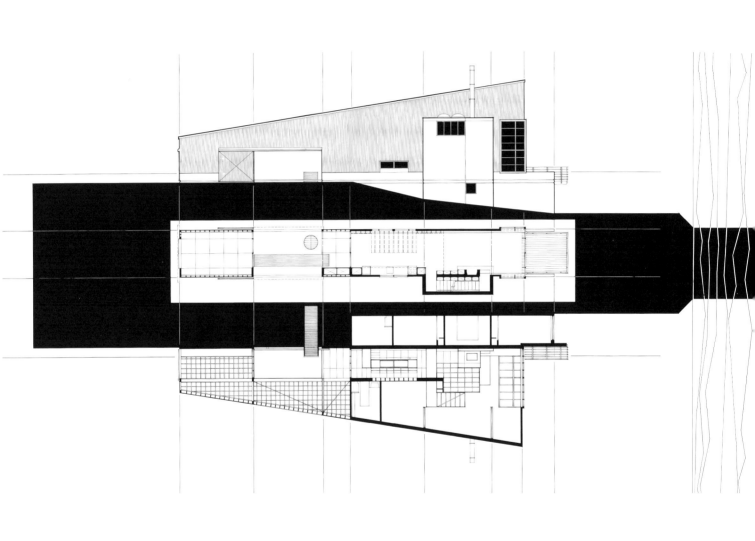

New Brunswick

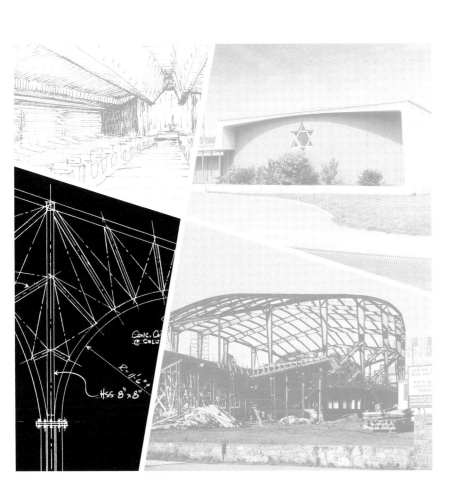

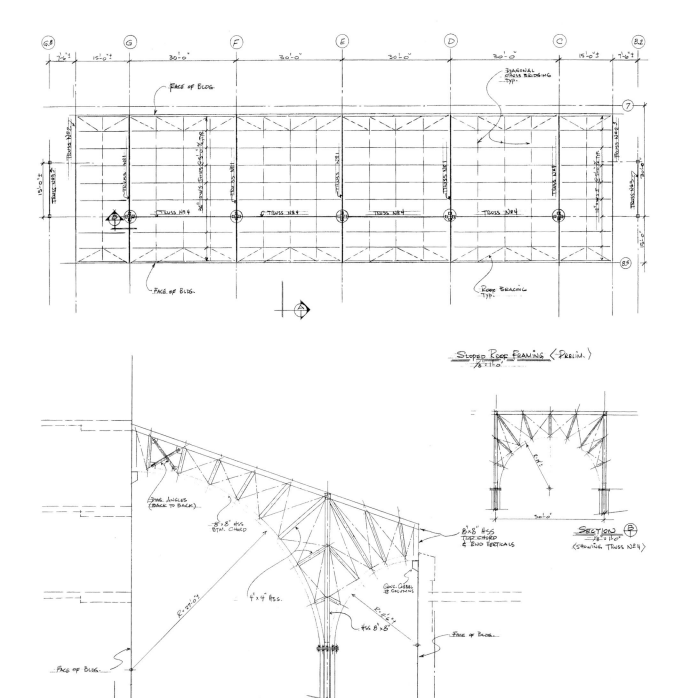

SLOPED ROOF FRAMING (PRELIM.)
1/8" = 1'-0"

SECTION B
1/8" = 1'-0"
(SHOWING TRUSS No 4)

SECTION A
1/4" = 1'-0"
(SHOWING TRUSS No 1)

FEB 23/87   HMS.
ARCHITECTS 4 LTD.

Blue Cross Centre

1987–1988
644 Main Street, Moncton, NB
Architectural firm: ARCOP Architects, Toronto, ON
Architectural firm: Architects Four Ltd., Moncton, NB
Principal architect: Robert Eaton
Design architects: Pierre Gallant, Paul Hughes, Andrew McGillivary

The downtown mixed-use complex is a characteristic project type of the 1980s, with examples in almost every city in Atlantic Canada. Usually intended as a spur to downtown revitalization, these projects combine large volumes of corporate office space with new facilities for an important public institution, typically a library. The Blue Cross Centre occupies a prominent site at one end of downtown Moncton. The complex is seen in the round, with frontage on Main Street, along Mechanic Street and wrapping around onto Commercial Street, towards the Petitcodiac River. The head of the complex is a three-storey block, with an eight-storey tower beyond; in between is a mid-block public galleria connecting Main and Commercial Streets, lined with shops and giving access to the public library at the rear of the complex and to the adjacent theatre building.

The building mass conforms to the traditional street pattern, with ground floor shops set tight to the street and offices above. Polychrome brick cladding with stone detailing reflects the traditional brick architecture of downtown Moncton, and the variegated massing invokes the spirit of blocks of nineteenth-century party-wall commercial buildings. The Centre is developed at the scale of the block rather than the lot, with only a few points of access, and the galleria accentuates its orientation inward, away from the street. A clock tower marks the bend in the axis of Main Street as well as the entry to the galleria. The historicist ambitions of the architecture are best expressed in the galleria roof, where the trussed steel supports are given a wonderful lightness of substance and expression rivalling that of Victorian train sheds.

38. *Plan layout and sections of galleria roof truss, design drawing, February 23, 1987. Delineator: HMS. Plastic lead on mylar. Architects Four collection.*
39. *Blue Cross Centre from Commercial Street. n.d. Architects Four collection.*
40. *Glazed roof and trusses at the galleria. n.d. Architects Four collection.*

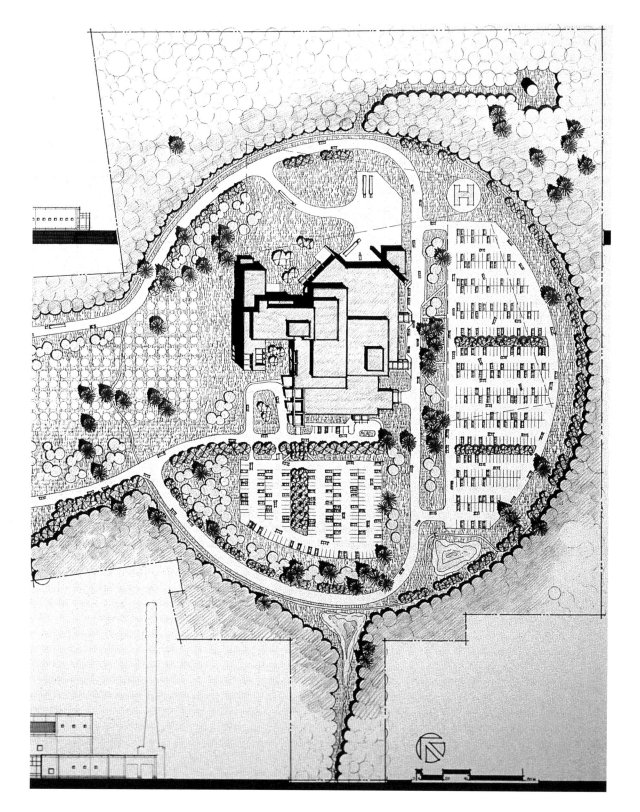

Miramichi Regional Hospital

1993–1996
500 Water Street, Chatham Head, NB
Architectural firm: Architects Four Ltd., Moncton, NB
Principal architect: Anthony Staples
Design architects: Pierre Gallant, Andrew McGillivary

Miramichi Regional Hospital is a new building on a clear site, a situation rarely occurring in contemporary hospital design, which almost inevitably involves piecemeal adaptation of existing buildings. As a result, rather than being constrained by existing built forms and the logistical demands of phasing to keep the hospital operating during construction, the Miramichi designers were able to conceive a fresh relation of form, site and function. The clear organization of the plan is sustained in the three-dimensional modeling of the massing. Two large brick volumes – one tall, one low – sandwich a glass prism reaching skyward. The effect of this play of simple forms against the distant line of trees is reminiscent of the powerful forms of pulp mills elsewhere in northern New Brunswick.

Clarity of organization and formal rigour are carried into the site planning as well. The irregular site boundary is given order by the creation of a circular clearing of trees encompassing the hospital and grounds. Driveways and parking are developed to suit this geometry. Generous portions of the site are developed as garden and landscape spaces for summer use, while a grand, glass-roofed canopy shelters a large entry plaza from the harsh winter weather.

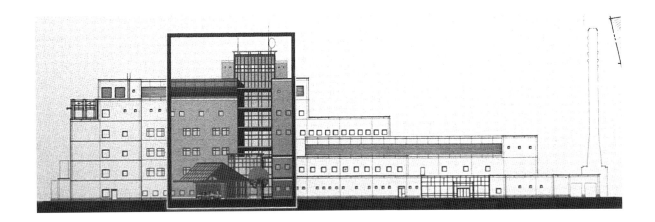

41. Site plan, detail of "The Miramichi Regional Hospital" presentation panel [not numbered], n.d. Mixed media and ink on illustration board. Architects Four collection.
42. Elevation, detail of "The Miramichi Regional Hospital" presentation panel [not numbered], n.d. Mixed media and ink on illustration board. Architects Four collection.

La Dune de Bouctouche: Irving Eco-Centre

1996–1997
Bouctouche, NB
Architectural firm: Architects Four Ltd. / Elide Albert Architect Ltd., Moncton, NB
Principal architect: Elide Albert
Design architect: Andrew McGillivary

The dune ecology centre is one of the anchor projects of the Bouctouche Bay Ecotourism Plan of 1996, which proposed an integrated model of ecologically-based regional development. The 12-kilometre-long dune of white sand that divides Bouctouche Bay from the Northumberland Strait is among the few undeveloped dunes in the northeast, and the position of the Eco-Centre at the meeting point of dune and mainland allows control and protection of the fragile landscape, as well as interpretation and enjoyment. A meandering 1.8-kilometre boardwalk occupies the high point of the dune, giving protected access to a sequence of six dune ecosystems: forest, salt marsh, pond, lagoon, marram grass, and beach.

At the mainland end of the boardwalk are a set of small-scale, single-room buildings housing an interpretive centre with interactive exhibits, an education centre for school visits, lectures and research, and a canteen building with public washrooms. A lookout tower offers a view of the full extent of the dune, while composting toilets and a greywater recycling system minimize the human impact. The board and shake walls and pyramidal wood shingle roofs evoke contemporary New England precedents more strongly than the local building traditions. These shingled volumes are placed loosely around a grand flight of wooden steps, which also serve as an informal outdoor theatre.

43. *Aerial view of site, n.d. J. D. Irving Co. collection.*
44. *Perspective view to entry pavilion, detail of "Buctouche [sic] Ecotourism Plan" presentation drawing [not numbered], May 7, 1996. Delineator: Andrew McGillivary. Ink on vellum. Architects Four collection.*
45. *Boardwalk, April 2001. Photographer: Chad Jamieson.*

Windsor Town Houses

1996
Westmorland at Brunswick Street, Fredericton, NB
Architectural firm: Goguen & Smyth Architecture and Planning, Fredericton, NB
Design architect: Carl Smyth

The traditional rowhouse is characteristic of nineteenth-century neighbourhoods in Atlantic Canadian cities. Its great attractions – individual ownership, no neighbours above or below to cause disturbance, and density of land use – are now most often expressed in the town house, which adds a parking space between street and front wall, making the house remote from the life of the street and giving the street entirely over to the car. The Windsor Town Houses project uses the straightforward wood frame construction of contemporary townhouses but pushes the front facade of the houses back out, tight to the street where they belong, restoring the intimacy between sidewalk and front door so essential to urban street life. Parking is tucked behind, in a paved court that can double as a paved and protected play area.

The individuality of each house is played up rhetorically in the massing. Typical townhouse construction has the roof ridge running the length of each row, a straightforward method of construction that presents a single long slope of shingles to the street. The Windsor Townhouses set the ridge perpendicular to the length of the row, providing each house with its own roof peak and gable end which express its individuality to the street.

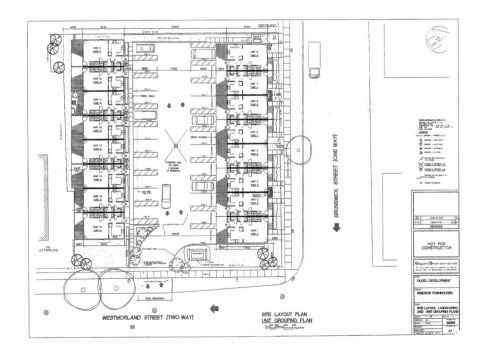

46. Line of gable ends along Brunswick Street. Goguen & Company collection.
47. "Site Layout, Landscaping and Unit Grouping Plans" planning permission drawing #96056-A1, February 24, 1997. Delineator: Kevin. CAD file. Goguen & Company collection.

Le Pays de la Sagouine

1991 / 1999
Bouctouche, NB / Ile-aux-Puces, NB
Architectural firm: Architects Four Ltd., Moncton, NB
Principal architect: Elide Albert / Dianne VanDommelen
Design architect: Jeff VanDommelen / Jeff VanDommelen

Restoration and reconstruction work became an important aspect of modern architecture in Canada in the 1960s, in projects such as the restoration of the Saint John City Market and the Historic Properties in Halifax, and in major historic reconstructions exemplified by the work at Fortress Louisbourg on Cape Breton. Pays de la Sagouine is a peculiar example of a "heritage" reconstruction – the physical embodiment of a fictional place formerly existing only in the words of Antonine Maillet's popular stories of the Acadian charwoman "La Sagouine."

Parking, reception, restrooms and boutiques, key components of any tourist architecture, were placed on the mainland in a first phase of building, along with an observation tower offering a view of the entire complex. From the tower a boardwalk snakes over the Bouctouche River to Ile-aux-Puces and the main village complex, constructed in the second phase. The high tidal range necessitated tall pilings for the boardwalk, which were driven during the winter freeze-over to minimize site disruption. The delicate dune-grass ecology of the site led to the village form, with roads and building sites determined by the pathways and clearings remaining from old farms on the island. The village is entirely elevated on a platform on piles, eliminating any need to disturb the marshland with fill.

That's what he wanted most, a big house, with a veranda all aroun' where he could sit on his rockin' chair all year long 'n' watch the people passin' by.
   - Antonine Maillet, "La Sagouine," trans. Luis de Cespides

What "La Sagouine" does through words, the architects have attempted to do through form and materials: interpret and celebrate the folklore and traditions of Acadie. The village includes two theatres for concerts and reenactments of the stories of "La Sagouine." Other buildings are drawn from the stories, including the houses of "La Sagouine" and "La Sainte," along with shops, smokehouses and bars. Buildings are of wood, stick and timber-frame construction atop the pile-supported platform. Their simple prismatic forms, clapboard and wood shingle surfaces, and mullioned windows are drawn from the traditional buildings of rural New Brunswick. The island lighthouse looks back to the observation tower on the mainland and stands as a more universal symbol of collective architectural memory.

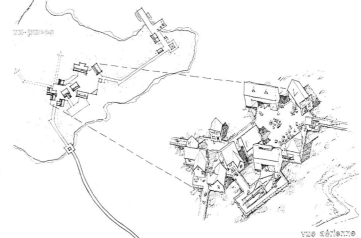

vue aérienne

48. The boardwalk, looking towards Ile-aux-Puces, n.d. Architects Four collection.
49. "vue aerienne" axonometric presentation drawing; detail of "Le Pays de la Sagouine" presentation panel [not numbered], n.d. Mixed media and photocopy on mylar. Architects Four collection.
50. (overleaf) "Washroom" design drawing [not numbered], n.d. Delineator: Jeff VanDommelen. Ink and coloured marker on tracing paper. Architects Four collection.
51. (overleaf) "Boutique" design drawing [not numbered], n.d. Delineator: Jeff VanDommelen. Ink and coloured marker on tracing paper. Architects Four collection.

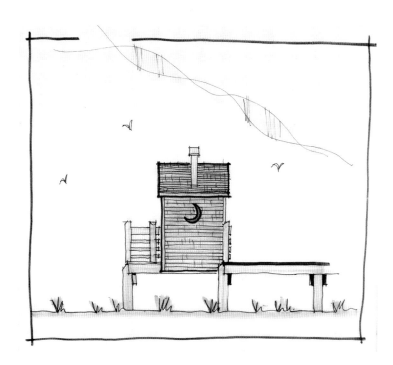

BOUTIQUE
1:50

Prince Edward Island

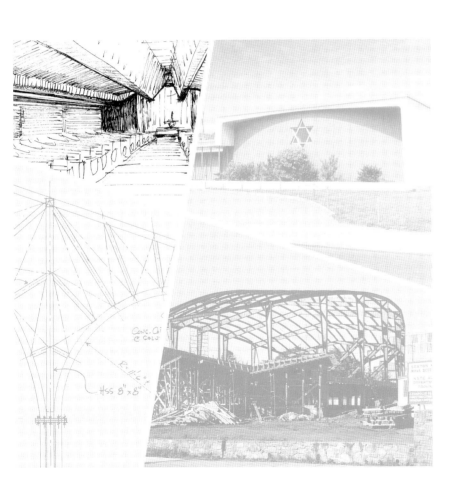

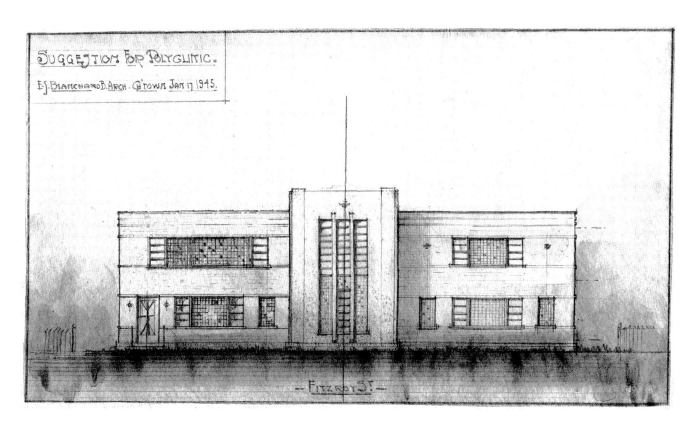

SUGGESTION FOR POLYCLINIC.

E.J. BLANCHARD B. ARCH. C'TOWN JAN 17 1945.

- FITZROY ST. -

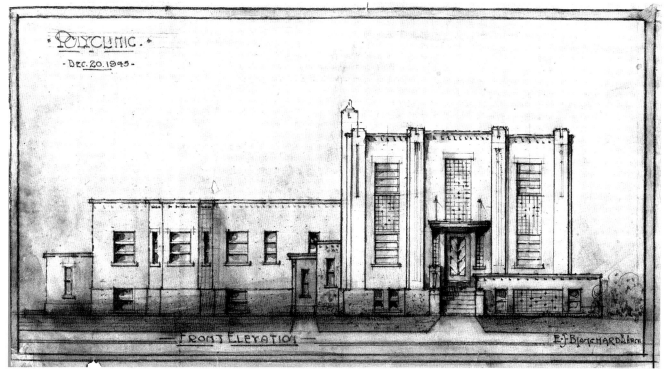

· POLYCLINIC ·

- DEC. 20. 1945 -

- FRONT ELEVATION -

E.J. BLANCHARD B. ARCH

Polyclinic

1945–1949
178 Fitzroy Street, Charlottetown, PE
Architectural firm: E. S. Blanchard Architect, Charlottetown, PE
Design architects: E. Stirling Blanchard, James F. Toombs

Polyclinic is the earliest project in the exhibition, and is very much a transitional design. The plan of the building is rooted in traditional nineteenth-century Beaux-Arts methods, involving a symmetrical placement of cellular rooms along clear axial corridors. The Polyclinic plan is produced by the crossing of two axes, with stairs and services placed at the intersection. In its exterior expression, the architects attempt ever so tentatively to break away from the dictates of symmetry, as can be seen in the series of studies for the front facade. The effort to shift the entry off centre appears to have been too compromising of the internal organization, while the sketch showing a symmetrical facade rendered in a "streamline" language remains dull and plodding. As built, the entrance remains on the central axis, but the building mass has been syncopated by a variety of heights and setbacks on each wing, and streamlined by the curved wall flanking the path to the doors. Inside, the reception counter curves echo the outer wall, but the plan beyond reverts to the traditional narrow corridors leading to ranges of cellular clinic rooms.

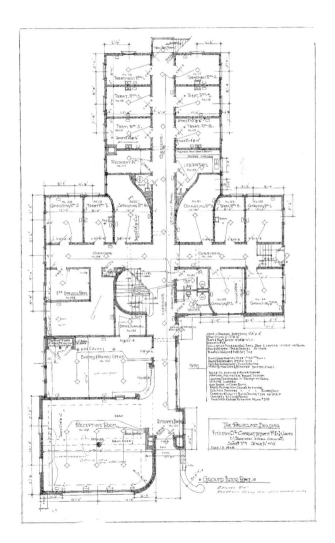

52. "Suggestion for Polyclinic" design presentation drawing, January 17, 1945 [1946]. Delineator: [E. S. Blanchard]. Pencil and watercolour on paper. Public Archives of Prince Edward Island collection.
53. "Polyclinic - Front Elevation" design presentation drawing, December 20, 1945. Delineator: [E. S. Blanchard]. Pencil and watercolour on tracing paper. Public Archives of Prince Edward Island collection.
54. View of entrance from Fitzroy Street, March 2001. Photographer: Chad Jamieson.
55. "Ground Floor Plan" contract drawing #4, May 15, 1948. Delineator: [E. S. Blanchard]. Pencil on vellum. Public Archives of Prince Edward Island collection.

Belvedere Golf and Winter Club, Clubhouse

1962–1963
1 Greensview Drive, Charlottetown, PE
Architectural firm: Alfred J. Hennessey Architect, Charlottetown, PE
Design architect: Alfred Hennessey

Belvedere Golf and Winter Club is a two-part building reflecting the very different characters of the two seasonal activities. A plain, boxy volume contains curling rinks, built of concrete block with only a few punched window openings and set squarely down on the ground. This wing divides the parking area from the golf course and acts as an anchor for the adjacent clubhouse wing. Joined to the rink volume by a glass-walled link, services for the clubhouse are contained in another plain box shape, this one lifted just above the ground by short posts. Breaking free from the end is the "belvedere" of the club rooms, entirely glass-walled and surrounded by a deep verandah. The verandah floor and canopy are expressed as strong horizontal elements, hovering on a cushion of deep shadow over the rippling grass surface of the golf course. Very dainty, widely spaced steel columns supporting the canopy provide a nominal gesture of enclosure to the verandah but do not detract from the powerful shadows that create its floating quality. The deeply incised joints of the dark-stained board siding underscore the horizontal theme and contrast the light, flat expression of the curling rink box.

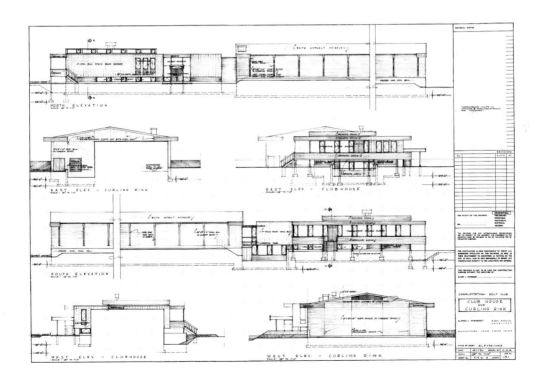

56. *View from the southeast, n.d. Public Archives of Prince Edward Island collection.*
57. *"Elevations" contract drawing #151-A-6, July 1962. Delineator: CHM [Claude Maurice]. Pencil and ink on vellum. Public Archives of Prince Edward Island collection.*

51

Holy Redeemer Roman Catholic Church

1962–1964
3 Pond Street, Charlottetown, PE
Architectural firm: Alfred J. Hennessey Architect, Charlottetown, PE
Design architect: Alfred Hennessey

The Redemptorist Fathers established a foundation to minister to west-end Charlottetown in 1929, beginning in a church basement and then building a tradition of social and spiritual activism. Alfred Hennessey was a member of the parish when he was commissioned to design a new church in the early 1960s. The design work began in late 1962, and the church was under construction the following year, with the first mass celebrated in July 1964. The form huddles close to the ground, a fan-shaped plan enclosed by low perimeter walls, covered by a prominent roof supporting an expressive spire. A masterful play of light and darkness animates the interior. Radial lines of shadow in the folded plate beams lead to a blast of tinted light beneath the central lantern. The rich, coarse textures of the brick interior walls and stone floor ripple in the light, while the ragged geometries of plan and section provide additional pools of darkness.

To early twenty-first-century eyes this appears to be a very typical Roman Catholic church. The timeline shows that Holy Redeemer is not merely typical, but rather is a prototype of the late twentieth-century church. Pope John XXIII called the Second Vatican Council to reinvigorate Catholic worship, proposing a new "biblical" (rather than "juridical") model for the church. The first session of the Council convened in October 1962, while the church was in design, and Hennessey says that "changes were made to the drawings as Vatican II was unfolding." The church as built embodies a fully developed architectural approach to the liturgical reforms of the Council: the celebrant priest is behind the altar, facing the congregation who sit in pews arranged for optimal view and participation in the mass, which is now in the vernacular rather than in Latin. The formal and liturgical innovations of Holy Redeemer Church have since become a commonplace of church architecture.

> *The old priest had to be gently dissuaded of the old ways. I remember describing to him the concept of the church: "When Christ was down on earth, people didn't line up in front of him in neat rows of pews. They gathered around him." That finally convinced him.*
>
> - Alfred Hennessey

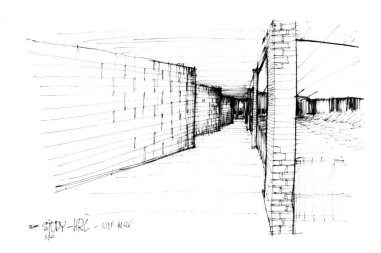

58. View of altar, April 2001. Photographer: Chad Jamieson.
59. "Study - HRC" design sketch, December 1, 1962. Delineator: Alfred Hennessey. Ink and pencil on tracing paper. Alfred Hennessey collection.

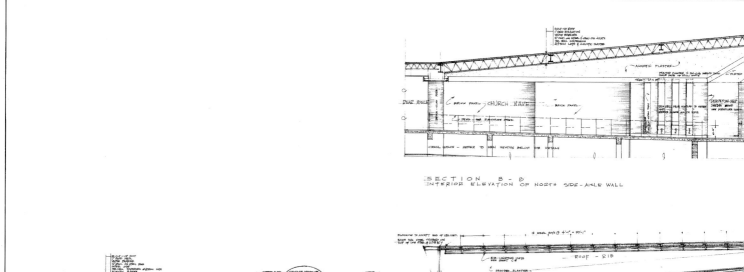

SECTION B - B
INTERIOR ELEVATION OF NORTH SIDE-AISLE WALL

MAIN LONGITUDINAL SECTION A - Z

WEEKDAY CHAPEL   NARTHEX   MAIN CHURCH

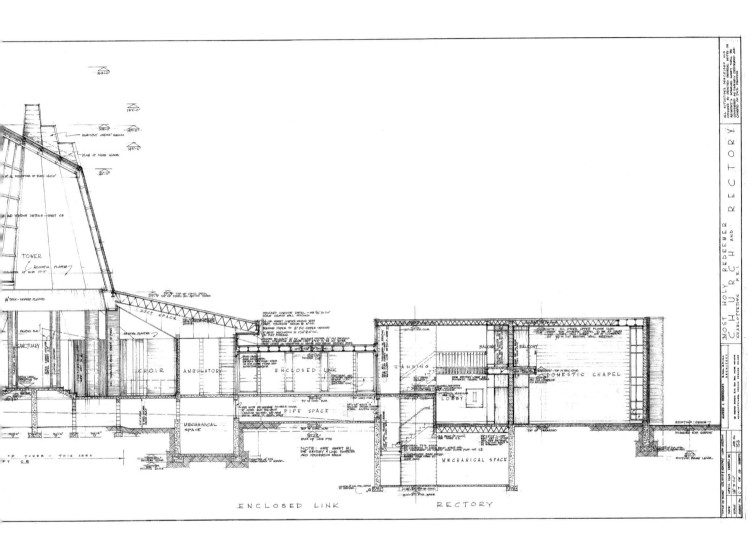

60. "Church and Rectory Long Section" contract drawing #153-C7, April 1963. Delineator: [Claude Maurice]. Pencil and ink on vellum. Public Archives of Prince Edward Island collection.

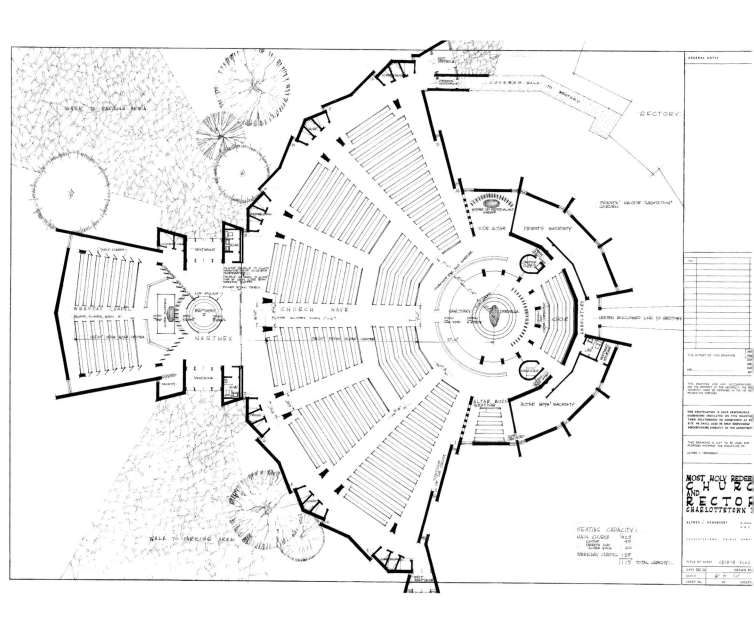

61. "Church Plan" design drawing [not numbered], December 1962. Delineator: CHM [Claude Maurice]. Black ink, sepia ink and pencil on vellum. Alfred Hennessey collection.

62. Exterior view towards entry and tower, April 2001. Photographer: Chad Jamieson.

63. "High Window: Elevations, Sliding Door Details, Weekday Chapel Screening Fins" contract drawing #153-C9, April 1963. Delineator: [Claude Maurice]. Pencil and ink on vellum. Public Archives of Prince Edward Island collection.

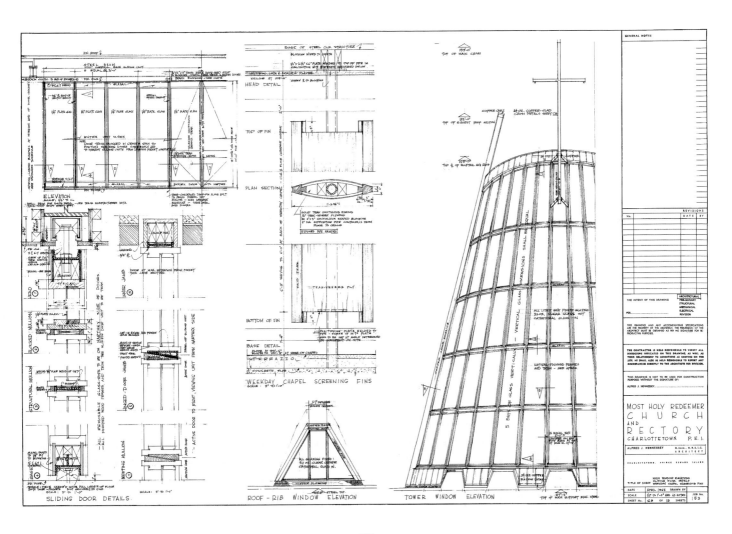

Central Creameries, New Production Plant

1966–1967
215 Fitzroy Street, Charlottetown, PE
Architectural firm: Keith Pickard Architect, Charlottetown, PE
Design architect: Keith Pickard

Central Creameries was a major force in the Maritimes dairy products industry and a large-scale producer of butter and evaporated milk. The firm was also responsible for construction of a number of well designed industrial buildings in Charlottetown. The New Production Plant for Central Creameries was built to handle ice cream production, and is a fine example of the virtues of care and attention in a modest design. The overall mass and plan of the creamery are quite simple, but the long wall surfaces are carefully composed with alternating planes of brick and glass. The building sits at a street intersection, with entrances held well back from the corner to allow a grand and uninterrupted curve of aluminum and glass curtain wall to wrap from one street to the other, making the two facades continuous. The building sits quite close to both streets, with parking and loading tucked away behind the building, making it a well-behaved part of its urban neighbourhood.

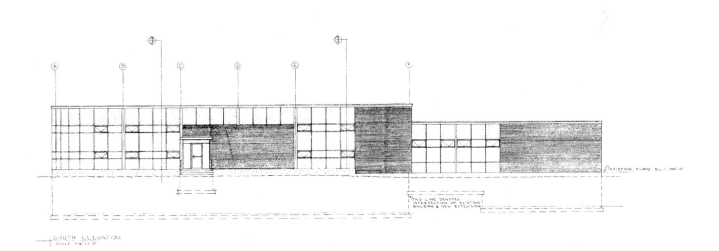

SOUTH ELEVATION

64. *Detail of curving curtain wall, southwest corner, April 2001. Photographer: Chad Jamieson.*
65. *Overall view, April 2001. Photographer: Chad Jamieson.*
66. *"Elevations" preliminary contract drawing #66-55-03, December 30, 1966. Delineator: RB. Diazoprint. Amalgamated Dairies Ltd. collection.*

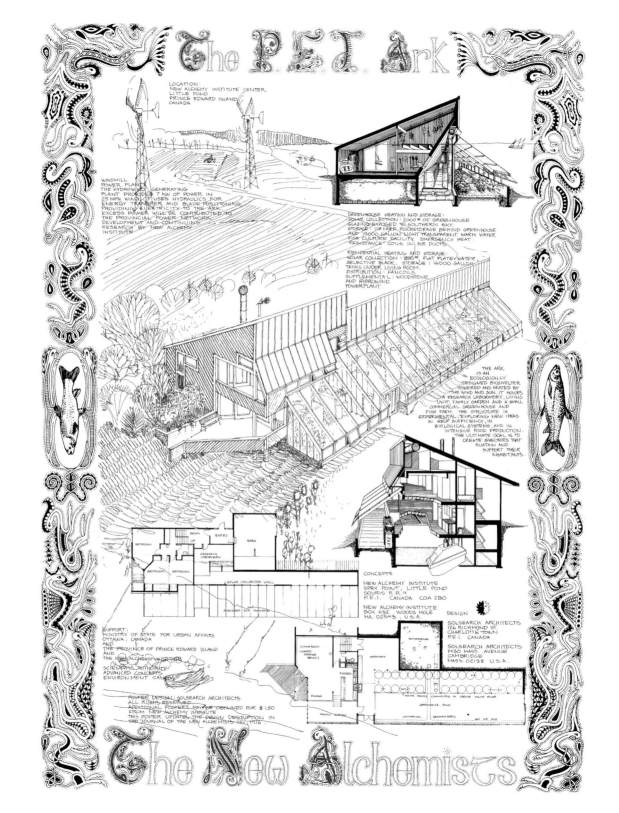

The P.E.I. Ark

LOCATION:
NEW ALCHEMY INSTITUTE CENTER
LITTLE POND
PRINCE EDWARD ISLAND
CANADA

WINDMILL
POWER PLANT
THE HYDROWIND GENERATING
PLANT PROVIDES 7 KW OF POWER IN
25 MPH WIND. IT USES HYDRAULICS FOR
ENERGY TRANSFER AND BLADE POSITIONING
PROVIDING ELECTRICITY TO THE ARK.
EXCESS POWER WILL BE CONTRIBUTED TO
THE PROVINCIAL POWER NETWORK.
DEVELOPMENT AND CONTINUING
RESEARCH BY NEW ALCHEMY
INSTITUTE.

GREENHOUSE HEATING AND STORAGE:
SOLAR COLLECTION: 2000 # OF GREENHOUSE
GLAZING EXPOSED TO SOUTHERN SKY.
STORAGE: 118 YARD ROCKSTORAGE BEHIND GREENHOUSE
AND 19000 GALLON LIGHT TRANSPARENT WARM WATER
FISH CULTURE FACILITY. EMERGENCY HEAT:
RESISTANCE COILS IN AIR DUCTS.

RESIDENTIAL HEATING AND STORAGE
SOLAR COLLECTION: 880 # FLAT PLATE/WATER
SELECTIVE BLACK. STORAGE: 16000 GALLON
TANKS UNDER LIVING ROOM.
DISTRIBUTION: FANCOILS.
SUPPLEMENTAL: WOODSTOVE
AND HYDROWIND
POWERPLANT.

THE ARK
IS AN
ECOLOGICALLY
DESIGNED BIOSHELTER
POWERED AND HEATED BY
THE WIND AND SUN. IT HOUSES
A RESEARCH LABORATORY, LIVING
UNIT, FAMILY GARDEN AND A SMALL
COMMERCIAL GREENHOUSE AND
FISH FARM. THE STRUCTURE IS
EXPERIMENTAL, EXPLORING NEW IDEAS
IN SELF SUFFICIENCY, IN
BIOLOGICAL SYSTEMS, AND IN
INTENSIVE FOOD PRODUCTION.
THE ULTIMATE GOAL IS TO
CREATE SHELTERS THAT
SUSTAIN AND
SUPPORT THEIR
INHABITANTS.

CONCEPTS

NEW ALCHEMY INSTITUTE
SPRY POINT, LITTLE POND
SOURIS R.R. 4
P.E.I. CANADA COA 2BO

NEW ALCHEMY INSTITUTE
BOX 432 WOODS HOLE
MA. 02543 U.S.A.

DESIGN

SOLSEARCH ARCHITECTS
126 RICHMOND ST.
CHARLOTTE TOWN
P.E.I. CANADA

SOLSEARCH ARCHITECTS
1430 MASS. AVENUE
CAMBRIDGE
MASS. 02138 U.S.A.

SUPPORT:
MINISTRY OF STATE FOR URBAN AFFAIRS
OTTAWA, CANADA
AND
THE PROVINCE OF PRINCE EDWARD ISLAND
AND
THE NEW ALCHEMY INSTITUTE

SCIENCE AUTHORITY
ADVANCED CONCEPTS
ENVIRONMENT CANADA

The New Alchemists

The PEI Ark

1975–1976
Spry Point, Little Pond, PE (demolished)
Architectural firm: Solsearch Architecture, Charlottetown, PE and Cambridge, MA
Design architects: David Bergmark, Ole Hammarlund

> *This Island ... is now providing hospitality to a new commit-*
> *ment, a commitment that the environmentalists refer to as*
> *"living lightly on the earth."*
>
> - Pierre Elliott Trudeau, at the opening of the PEI Ark

The PEI Ark began as an "urban demonstration project" of sustainable building systems funded by the Canadian Department of Urban Affairs for the 1976 United Nations Habitat Conference. Conceived by the New Alchemy Institute, a Boston-based group (linked to the Woods Hole Oceanographic Institute) devoted to a renewed integration of science and the humanities, the Ark was powered by sun and wind, grew its own food on the grounds and in its greenhouse, and was intended to be fully self-sufficient on its remote rural site. Labs and living quarters supported the Ark as a full-scale, real-time experiment in living. David Bergmark became involved in the architectural realization of the Ark through a chance meeting with Dr. John Todd of the New Alchemists. Just a year out of architecture school, Bergmark established a partnership with Ole Hammarlund on the promise of the Ark. Bergmark moved to the Island first to oversee construction, then with his young family to live in the

experiment for its first year and to monitor the operation of the solar heating and ventilation system, the wind power generation, and the composting toilets.

The Ark's vision of the future was ambivalent at best. It was conceived at a time of enormous optimism and appetite for the future in Canada, and was officially opened by Prime Minister Pierre Trudeau, the country's paragon of social progress. The role of institutions and government in its inception would suggest the progressive potential of society. On the other hand, the remote site and the emphasis on self-sufficiency and closed systems suggest a contradictory rejection of organized social forms in a retreat to complete autonomy. Indeed "The Ark" was so called because the project was designed to survive what John Todd saw as the coming economic holocaust. Other urban refugees moved to the rural Maritimes in the 1970s based on their estimation of the fallout patterns from a nuclear strike on the U.S. eastern seaboard. In this contradiction the Ark reflects the unresolved motives of the back-to-the-land movement, attempting to build an Arcadian utopia while securing an escape from the coming technological apocalypse.

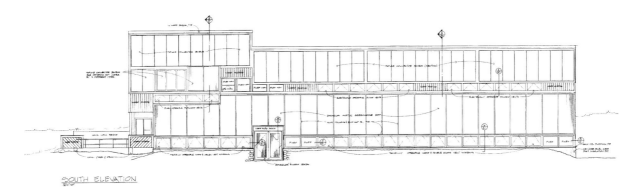

SOUTH ELEVATION

67. "The PEI Ark: The New Alchemists" poster, n.d. [1976]. Two-colour lithograph. Bergmark Guimond Hammarlund Jones collection.
68. "South Elevation" presentation drawing, n.d. [1976]. Delineators: [David Bergmark, Ole Hammarlund]. Ink and plastic lead on mylar. Bergmark Guimond Hammarlund Jones collection.

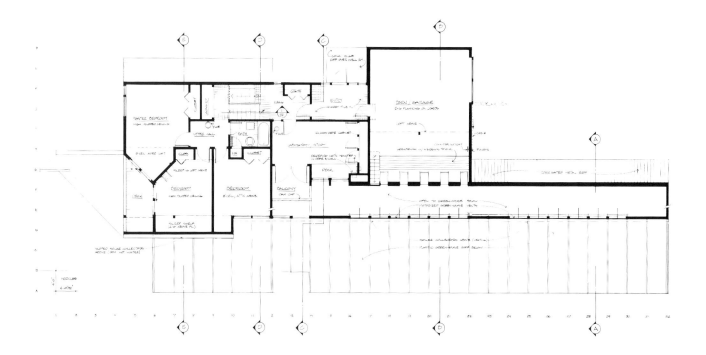

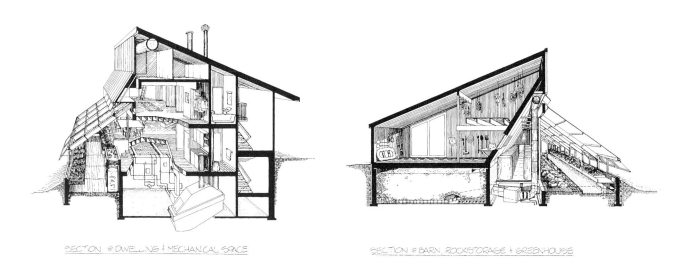

SECTION @ DWELLING & MECHANICAL SPACE

SECTION @ BARN, ROCKSTORAGE & GREENHOUSE

69. "Upper Level Plan" presentation drawing, n.d. [1976]. Delineators: [David Bergmark, Ole Hammarlund]. Ink on mylar. Bergmark Guimond Hammarlund Jones collection.

70. "Section Perspectives" presentation drawing, n.d. [1976]. Delineators: [David Bergmark, Ole Hammarlund]. Ink on mylar. Bergmark Guimond Hammarlund Jones collection.

71. *David Bergmark and Ole Hammarlund in front of the south wall and solar collector panels, n.d. Bergmark Guimond Hammarlund Jones collection.*

72. *Dr. John Todd of The New Alchemy Institute and Prime Minister Pierre Trudeau at the official opening of the PEI Ark, from "Trudeau Officially Opens Ark at Spry Point,"* Summerside Journal-Pioneer, *vol. 111, no. 290, September 22, 1976, page 1. News clipping. Public Archives of Prince Edward Island collection.*

Trudeau Officially Opens Ark At Spry Point

CHARLOTTETOWN — Before a crowd of 300 people Prime Minister Trudeau officially opened the wind and sun operated bio-shelter — the Ark. During his visit to Spry Point Tuesday afternoon the Prime Minister toured the building and met with local people. Later in the afternoon he met with fishermen in Bothwell and held a brief news conference in Charlottetown before he departed for New Brunswick.

Alfred Hennessey Residence

1980
74 Goodwill Avenue, Charlottetown, PE
Architectural firm: Alfred J. Hennessey Architect, Charlottetown, PE
Design architect: Alfred Hennessey

Alfred Hennessey's own house was designed during the time of fuel shortages and rising energy costs of the 1970s. The tight volume, the intricate internal planning and above all the expression through carefully composed surfaces stand in distinct contrast to the architect's designs of the early 1960s for Holy Redeemer Church and the Belvedere Club, which are much more freely planned and expressive in their play of volumes. The principle of "thermo-siphoning" drove the development of the house form. Thermo-siphoning is a double-skin approach to enclosure, with a continuous air circulation chamber between an inner and outer shell, controlled by dampers and shutters, and a two-storey greenhouse on the south side of the house. Solar heat from the greenhouse would rise to circulate between the two shells, pushing cooler air ahead of it and back to the greenhouse to be heated. Like the PEI Ark a few years earlier, but in a much more low-key fashion, the house was intended as a living experiment. Hennessey made research trips to study other thermo-siphon houses in Colorado and the Canadian Rockies, and actively monitored the performance of the house. "I got in between the walls and lit a cigarette just to see where the smoke would go, and sure enough it did [circulate] but very slowly."

The architect-owner also acted as general contractor, and the drawings show the design evolving throughout the building period, with changes made in response to site conditions and construction opportunities. Most working drawings (including Hennessey's of Holy Redeemer and Belvedere) are a definitive prediction of the final form of the building; Hennessey's drawings of the house are a remarkable document of the time and process of building and conceiving the house, as well as a description of its substance. The study model is evidence of the architect's passion for miniatures, which is expressed more fully in his extensive collection of flying model airplanes.

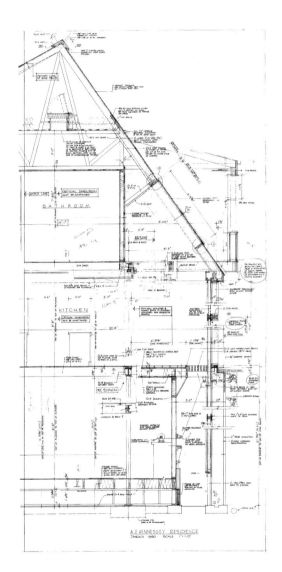

73. *View of house from the southwest, April 2001. Photographer: Chad Jamieson.*
74. *Wall section, construction drawing [not numbered], January 1980. Delineator: Alfred Hennessey. Pencil on yellow tracing paper. Alfred Hennessey collection.*

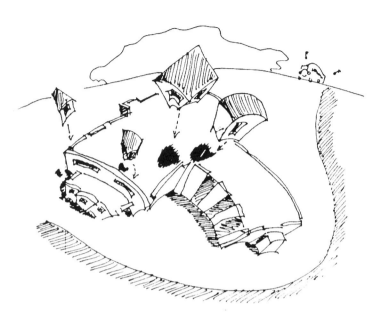

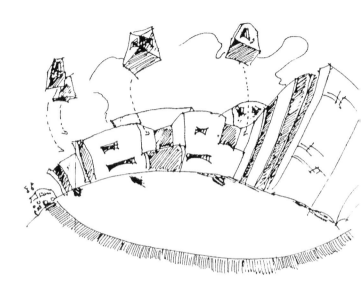

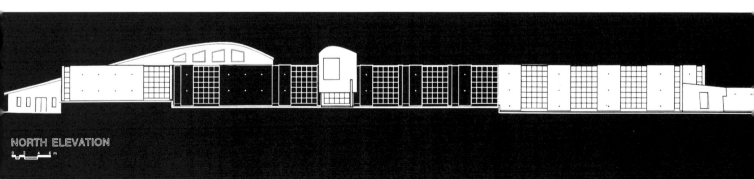

NORTH ELEVATION
0 2 4 6 m

Charlottetown Rural High School

1992–1994
100 Burns Crescent, Charlottetown, PE
Architectural firm: Bergmark & Hammarlund Architects, Charlottetown, PE
Design architect: David Bergmark

In the early 1960s an infusion of federal government funds triggered a major school building effort on Prince Edward Island. Schools were amalgated, and new schools built to suit new and progressive ideas in education. At the instigation of the province's premier, the four island architects – Laurie Coles, Alfred Hennessey, Peter MacNeil and Keith Pickard – formed Consortium Designers to ensure that the design work remained within the province. Charlottetown Rural High School was designed by Alfred Hennessey in 1964, and Hennessey also designed an extension in 1966. The original design was a classic example of 1960s school design, with plenty of natural light, generous corridors and an emphasis on building systems.

By 1990, the condition of the school had deteriorated severely, resulting in protests by students and parents. In contrast to Hennessey's concern for systems and order, David Bergmark's approach to the renewal of the school seeks to establish character and figures within the architecture. The courtyard space of the original design was roofed over to create a major new interior room, animated by a series of architectural figures clad in stucco. Other architectural figures populate the exterior of the building, marking entrances and important interior spaces. The aspirations for these figures show clearly in Bergmark's cartoons of the renovation process; their

eccentric shapes and strong colours take excellent advantage of their contrast with the cool reserve of the brick and window system of the original fabric.

David Bergmark's collaborator on the design of the renovation was John Watson, a TUNS graduate who died tragically young in Bermuda a few years later.

75, 76, 77 & 79 (overleaf). Sketches and elevations, details of presentation drawing [not numbered], n.d. [1992]. Delineator: [David Bergmark]. PMT print. Bergmark Guimond Hammarlund Jones collection.
78. View of entry facade, April 2001. Photographer: Chad Jamieson.

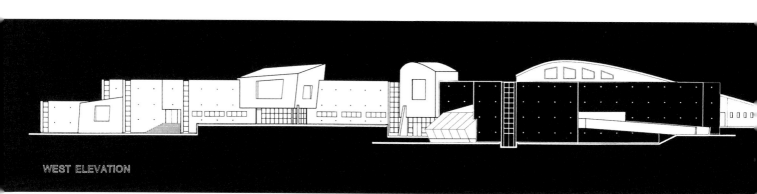

WEST ELEVATION

Newfoundland

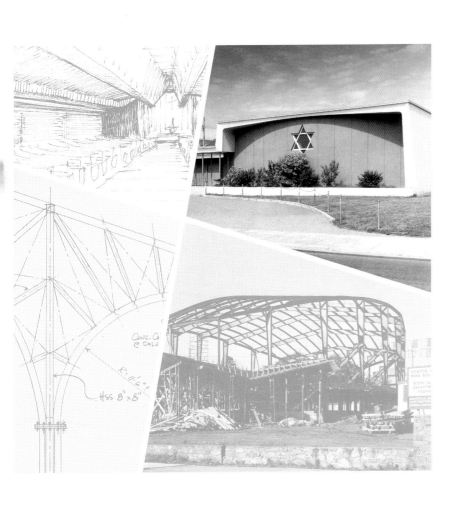

BETH-EL SYNAGOGUE

The Jewish Temple being so rich in tradition and symbolism the design of this synagogue presented quite a challenge. Among the symbols attributed to the synagogue and incorporated into this design are: the growing tree (The Tree of Life); the eight steps to the portico, (the eight main Holy Days of the year); the seven rows of portico columns (The Menorah, the Seven Branched Candlestick). The star of David, which is the predominant symbol is liberally incorporated into the windows, doors and floor details.

The total cost of the Beth-El Synagogue was $113,650.00.

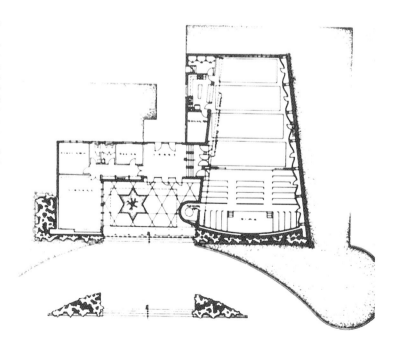

Beth-El Synagogue

1956–1959
128 Elizabeth Avenue, St. John's, NL
Architectural firm: Cummings & Campbell, Architects & Engineers, St. John's, NL
Design architect: Angus Campbell

Beth-El Synagogue forms a compact and urbane refuge on a major arterial road in what was a newly developed suburb of St. John's. Angus Campbell's own description of the project details the symbolic programme embodied in the design, which includes the tree of life in the entry court; the eight steps up to the portico, each representing a major holy day; and the seven pairs of portico columns, reflecting the seven candlesticks of the menorah.

Many nuances of the design reflect Campbell's deep study of the work of Frank Lloyd Wright. Most obvious is the intersection of the portico fascia with the battered fin wall fronting the office wing and its custom lettered sign, a composition based on passages of Wright's Taliesin West. The generous scale of Beth-El's automobile drop-off, crossed by an equally grand pedestrian stair, is compressed by the steps rising below the portico soffit, then released upwards in the entry court, only to be squeezed again in the vestibule. This play of compression and release is a typical Wrightian device, and delivers a sense of scale far grander than the actual size of the building and site would suggest. Beth-El is typical of Campbell's work in the use of a decorative motif developed in the window mullion arrangement, paving pattern, decorative paneling, and door design. Here the device is an extended, intersecting Star of David lattice; scaled up to fill the rear wall of the sanctuary, this lattice provides a monumental play of light and shadow to the worship space.

80. "Beth-El Synagogue" presentation page from Cummings & Campbell firm brochure, n.d. Photographer: Garland Studio. Offset print on paper. Angus Campbell collection.
81 & 82. Rear wall of sanctuary showing Star of David lattice, 1958; View of courtyard, 1958. Photographer: Max Fleet. From Gerald A. Davies, "Churches and Contemporary Architecture," RAIC Journal, vol. 35, no. 10 (Nov. 1958): 421. Sexton Design and Technology Library.

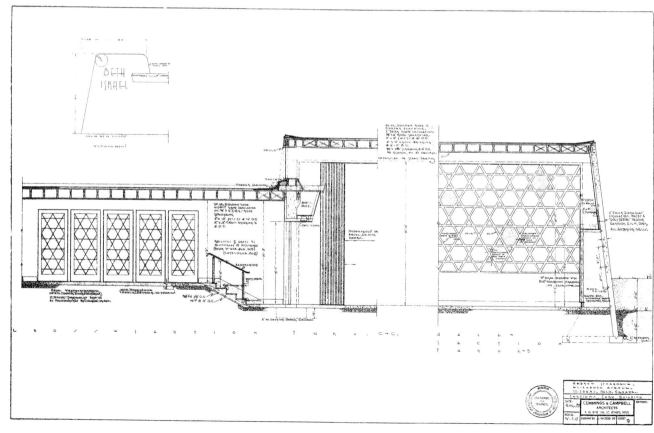

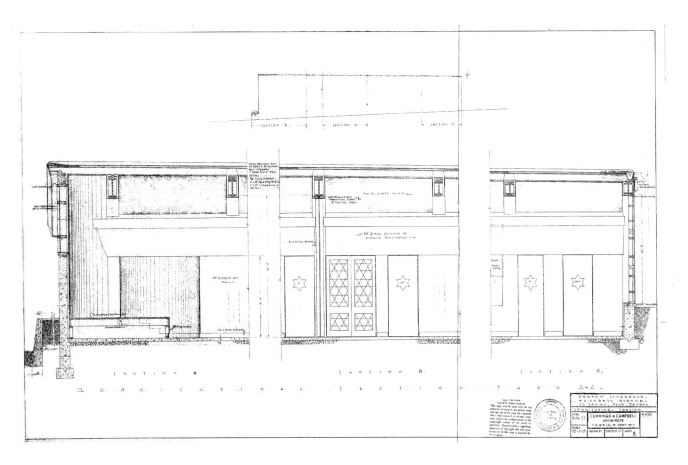

83. *Signage and canopy, 2000. Photographer: Ned Pratt. Ned Pratt collection.*
84. *"Sections Thru' Building" contract drawing #9, August 1957. Delineator: [Angus Campbell]. Inkjet print on vellum from scan of diazoprint. City of St. John's Archives collection.*
85. *"Longitudinal Section" contract drawing #8, August 1957. Delineator: [Angus Campbell]. Inkjet print on vellum from scan of diazoprint. City of St. John's Archives collection.*
86. *Elizabeth Avenue elevation showing wall and Star of David window to bimah, 2000. Photographer: Ned Pratt. Ned Pratt collection.*

SMALLWOOD'S PALATIAL HOME IS 60 MILES FROM THE CAPITAL. HIS STUDY IS IN A SUNKEN SECOND LIVING-ROOM BELOW THIS RAILING.

Newfoundland House (Joey Smallwood Residence)

1958–1960
Roaches Line, NL
Architectural firm: Cummings & Campbell, Architects & Engineers, St. John's, NL
Design architect: Angus Campbell

Commissioned by Premier Joey Smallwood as part of his controversial Russwood Ranch pig farm, Newfoundland House commands a prominent view across a reflecting pond from Roaches Line, and by its siting was long an inescapable landmark on the route from St. John's to the summer vacation area of Conception Bay South, or CBS. Joey erected a horse statue on a promontory opposite the house, while a gas station and restaurant across the road provided travelers with an ideal Joey-viewing point. The house was filled with gifts of tribute to the last Father of Confederation from industrial, mining and development interests. Much of this tribute is built into the fabric of the house, including the decorative tiles above the fireplace, gifts from a U.S. talc mining operation. Smallwood intended that the house be used after his death as a summer guest house for the premier and lieutenant-governor. It was deeded to the province for a dollar in 1962, but was returned to the Smallwood family in 1990 after years of neglect.

The plan is among the most geometrically adventurous in the work of Angus Campbell, also known in St. John's as "Angles" Campbell. The prow of the "vee" plan contains the living room, with its monumental fireplace crowned by a folded plate ceiling at the main level. An open well leads down to Joey's basement library and his collection of Wesleyana and Newfoundland history. Branching back from the prow are two wings enclosing a roughly pentagonal exterior court. These wings differ very slightly in floor area, some say a subtle symbol (by Campbell, or Smallwood himself?) of the 51% to 49% split in the 1949 referendum vote on Confederation with Canada.

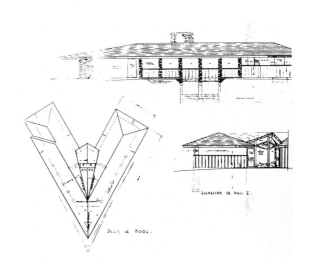

87. "Smallwood's palatial home is 60 miles from the capital." Photographer: Bob Brooks. From James Y. Nichol, "Pugnacious Joey: The whirling dervish from Newfoundland," The Star Weekly, Toronto (April 22, 1961): 8-9. Toronto Reference Library collection.
88. Detail of "Newfoundland House" presentation page from Cummings & Campbell firm brochure, n.d. Offset print on paper. Angus Campbell collection.

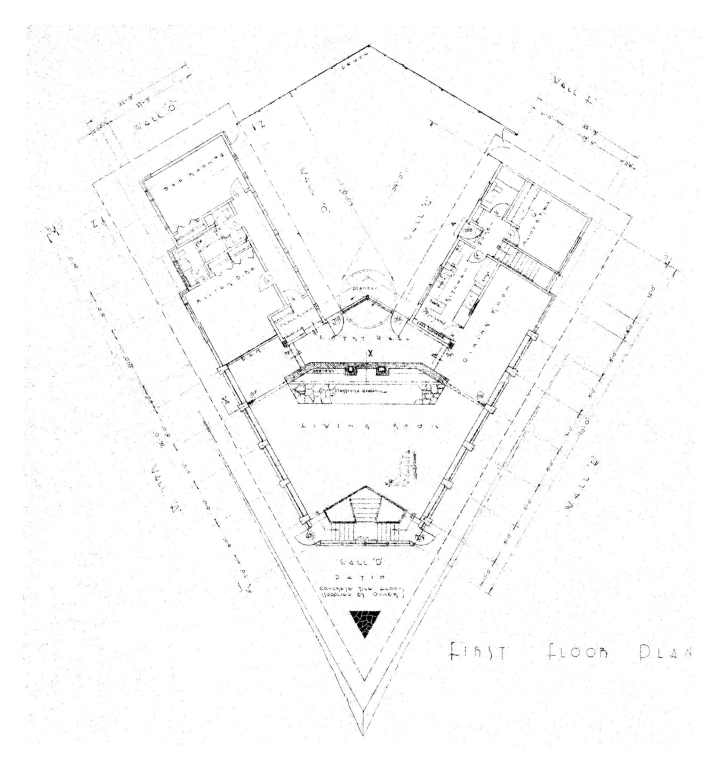

FIRST FLOOR PLAN

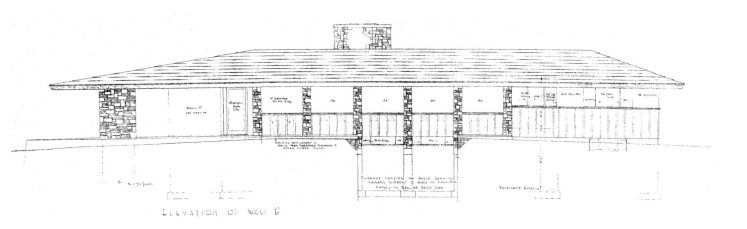

ELEVATION OF WALL C

89. Detail of "First Floor Plan" contract drawing #3, June 1958. Delineator: Angus Campbell. Sepia print. Angus Campbell collection.
90. Detail of "Elevations" contract drawing #5, June 1958. Delineator: Angus Campbell. Sepia print. Angus Campbell collection.
91. "Newfoundland House" painting by Reginald Shepherd, 1964. Oil on canvas. William Smallwood collection.

St. Bride's College, Littledale

1964–1966
250 Waterford Bridge Road, St. John's, NL
Architectural firm: Bolton, Ellwood & Aimers, Montreal, QC and Ottawa, ON
Associate architects: Horwood, Campbell & Guihan, St. John's, NL
Consultant: A. T. Galt Durnford, FRAIC, RCA, Montreal, QC

Adjacent to the nineteenth-century St. Bride's College, the new complex is nestled low into the hill, in contrast to the upright thrust of the original building. The new St. Bride's College develops the antique architectural form of the cloister in a modern language of concrete and glass. An irregular wall of low buildings is arranged around a long court, loosely divided in two by a tall chapel building and bell tower. Entry to the cloister is by way of a grand stair beneath a bridge that connects the chapel to the nuns' quarters; doors to all parts of the college open off the cloister. Various elements of the college are given distinct architectural expression. Classrooms and dormitories are clad in ribbed concrete panels with narrow windows, creating a staccato vertical rhythm reflecting the cellular planning within. Collective public rooms, including the dining hall and library, are sheltered by the loping curves of shallow concrete vaults, with large glass walls onto the cloister. The rooms beneath the vaults begin as double-height spaces, which are then richly developed in section; the mezzanine study room of the library, nestled up into the vaults and overlooking the tall reading room, is particularly fine.

The exterior of the college is almost entirely cast-in-place concrete, but the carefully studied variations in surface texture and the rhythm of openings give a rich range of expression. The interest in giving texture to concrete through manipulation of the wooden forms and the play of the shallow open vaults against rough-textured wall surfaces show the influence of the late work of Le Corbusier. Contrasting panels of dark red brick animate the end walls of the chapel, and cubic plinths of the brick mark out the various entry doors leading from the cloister. Within, the chapel is a masterpiece of spatial sequence and material expression. A pocket-sized vestibule dominated by a cubic stone baptismal font erupts into the tall worship room. The arcaded concrete structure is given a liner of red brick on the walls, which glows in the highly polished concrete floor. The brick walls, laminated wood beams and the wood tongue-and-groove mill deck ceiling create a very warm visual and acoustic space, enhanced by custom designed fixtures and wood pews.

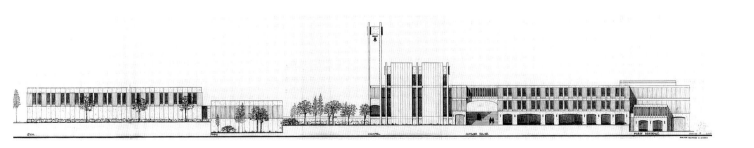

92. *Aerial view of the complex, n.d. Photographer: Doxco, photo #6407-E5761. Sisters of Mercy collection.*
93. *Elevation study of south wing: gymnasium, chapel and motherhouse, presentation drawing #6407-15, n.d. Ink on vellum. Collection: National Archives of Canada/ Archives Nationales du Canada, H. L. Fetherstonhaugh Fonds.*

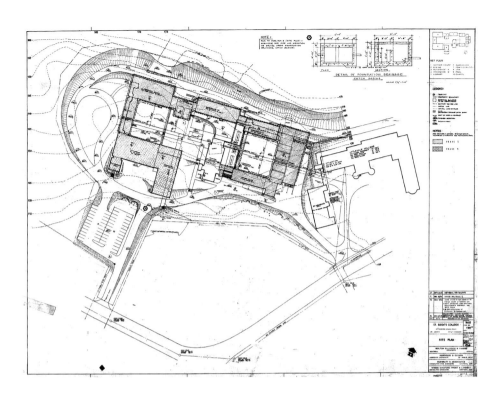

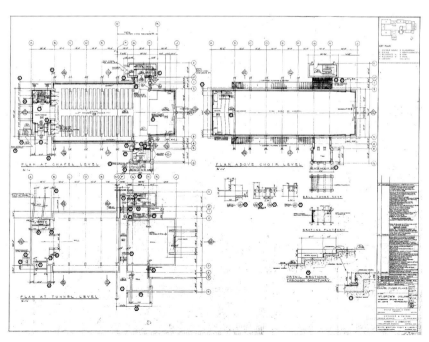

94. "Site Plan" contract drawing #6407-1:01D, March 23, 1965. Delineator: JCH. Ink on vellum. Collection: National Archives of Canada/ Archives Nationales du Canada, H. L. Fetherstonhaugh Fonds.

95. "Plan" contract drawing #6407-2-21F, September 30, 1965. Delineator: STA. Ink on vellum. Collection: National Archives of Canada/ Archives Nationales du Canada, H. L. Fetherstonhaugh Fonds.

96. Exterior of chapel, April 2001. Photographer: Chad Jamieson.

97. Concrete formwork for the dormitory wing during construction, October 1, 1965. Photographer: Tootons. Sisters of Mercy collection.

98. Font in the chapel vestibule, April 2001. Photographer: Chad Jamieson.

SUBJECT   ST. BRIDE'S COLLEGE
GENERAL CONTRACTOR J.I.E. PRICE & CO. (NFLD.) LTD.
DATE   OCTOBER 1st. 1965

Marine Sciences Research Laboratory

1964–1967
Logy Bay, NL
Architectural firm: Dobush, Stewart, Bourke, Holtshousen, St. John's, NL
Design architect: Peter Holtshousen
Executive architect: Sir Christopher Barlow

*If you want to be a marine biologist, you might as well do it
from a rock in the mid-Atlantic.*

- Dr. Frederick A. Aldrich, founding director

Early promotional material calls the Marine Sciences Research Laboratory an "outer space building for inner space research." The lab was founded to instigate leading research into cold water marine science. The site on Logy Bay had been a fisheries preserve since 1904, and sits adjacent to the mingling of the warm Gulf Stream and the cold Labrador Current. A key innovation of the lab strategy was to draw seawater directly from the bay for research purposes, and the management of water distribution is intimately linked to the extraordinary built form. According to Peter Holtshousen, the "facility was required to function 24 hours a day, 365 days a year, hence the central core with all services accessible. [The] concept reminded Aldrich of the sea anemone, which he promoted as his idea."

Aldrich's reading of the design has persisted, entwining symbol with process in the story of the building. The sea anemone has a single intestinal opening, the septa, simultaneously anus and mouth, leading to its intestinal tract, surrounded by a chambered body. The lab's gut is the central concrete core providing vertical circulation up from base for both researchers and seawater, ringed by 28 lab spaces forming a twelve-sided outer wall. The core is topped by the glass-enclosed phylarium. Here seawater flows into a ten-foot-diameter pool in which algae and plankton are grown, the fundamentals of

marine life. The water and food moves by gravity to the labs below, which study increasingly more complex forms of marine life as the distance from the phylarium increases.

The lab volumes ringing the core are concrete, clad in vertical wood board and batten siding, with horizontally pivoting porthole windows. The concrete structure is revealed by lugs projecting like spines through the wood siding at the angles. In the harsh marine conditions, the wood siding has weathered much better than the exposed concrete. Holtshousen's design proposed two additional lab pavilions of the same form for future expansion, linked by bridges. While subsequent architects picked up on the materials and details of the original, the building masses are much more conventional, and the complex has lost much of its original marvel.

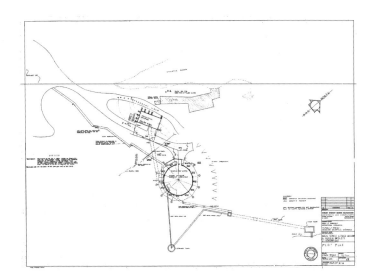

99. View up the boat ramp from Logy Bay, n.d. [1967]. Memorial University of Newfoundland Ocean Sciences Centre collection.
100. "Plot Plan" contract drawing #N6502-A1, February 25, 1966. Delineator: WJR. Sepia print. Memorial University of Newfoundland Facilities Management collection.

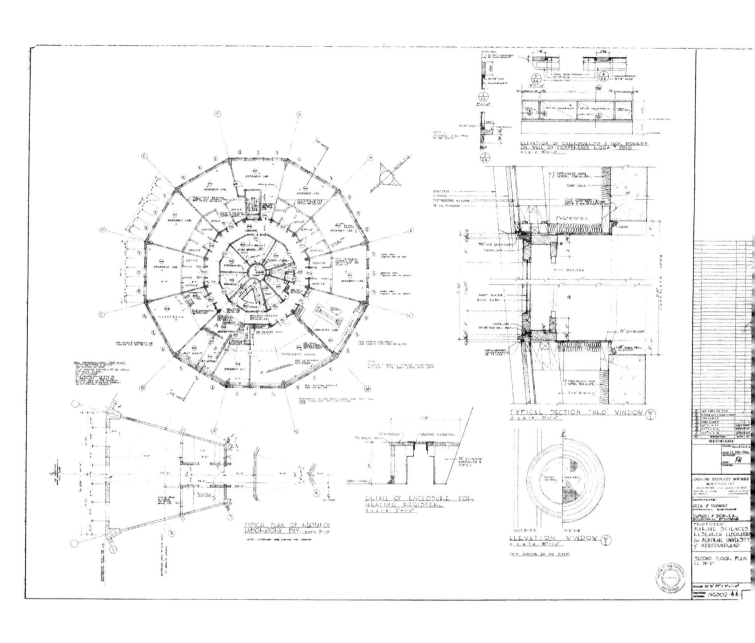

101. "Second Floor Plan, El. 74'-2" contract drawing #6502-A4R, February 25, 1966. Delineators: GK, WJR. Sepia print. Memorial University of Newfoundland Facilities Management collection.

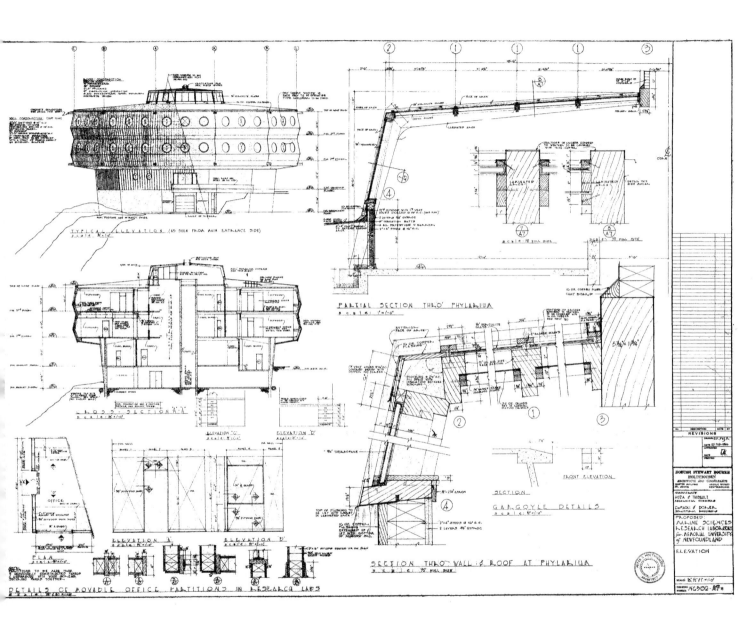

102. "Elevation" contract drawing #6502-A4R, February 25, 1966. Delineators: GK, WJR. Sepia print. Memorial University of Newfoundland Facilities Management collection.

Port aux Basques Interpretive Centre

1976–1978
Trans-Canada Highway, Port aux Basques, NL
Architectural firm: Beaton Sheppard Ltd., St. John's, NL
Design architect: Beaton Sheppard

This pavilion was conceived as a gateway to Newfoundland for visitors arriving on the ferry from Sydney, as the start of the eastbound Newfoundland leg of the Trans-Canada Highway, and also as a gateway for travelers heading north along the west coast of the island. The Minister of Tourism of the day began with an unequivocal image for the project: a giant wigwam, eighty feet high, which would honour the lost Beothuk heritage of the region. Beaton Sheppard's study of the regional landscape was more attuned to the rock formations of the fjords and cliffs, to the icebergs offshore, and especially to the characteristic built forms of the region, the sheds and leans that hunkered low against the prevailing high winds. The design was developed through model study, leading to an abstract crystalline form that recalls rock and iceberg, but also roof forms and sail shapes. A carefully orchestrated presentation to the Minister, in which his deputy (and arch-nemesis) pretended to support the wigwam scheme, inspired the Minister himself to favour this design instead.

The architects prepared a large framing model to supplement the drawings and assist the local builders in carrying out the construction. At the same time, Sheppard's office designed a small fleet of baby versions using the same vocabulary of forms and construction techniques, which serve as visitors' centres in Clarenville, Deer Lake and Whitbourne.

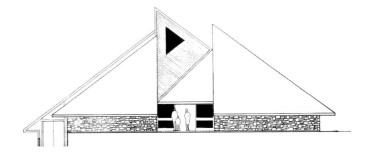

103. View from across driveway, n.d. [1978]. Beaton Sheppard collection.
104. Front elevation, n.d. PMT. Beaton Sheppard collection.
105. Framing model, n.d. [1978]. Modelmaker: Beaton Sheppard. Detail of mixed media on matte board presentation panel. Beaton Sheppard collection.

Forest Road Non-Profit Housing

1981–1983
179–229 Forest Road, St. John's, NL
Architectural firm: Sheppard, Burt, Pratt & Short, St. John's, NL
Design architect: Philip Pratt

Although it is entirely new construction on a greenfield suburban site, the Forest Road project was key to the subsequent development of a very aggressive urban infill approach that remains the policy of the City of St. John's Housing Department. The project followed a study by Philip Pratt, "Infill Housing Opportunities in St. John's," which aimed to completely transform the image of public housing, counter to the negative associations of the federally-funded high-rise, high-density projects of the 1960s. Working in parallel to Pratt's architectural and urban study, David Blackmore of the Housing Department and Councillor (later Mayor) Shannie Duff developed the necessary public policy and rallied popular support.

The Forest Road project embodies a generosity of accommodation and a desire for recognizable house forms, while taking advantage of its sloping site using strategies of early modern architecture. Staggered plans and sections of the townhouse blocks lend each dwelling a sense of identity while creating privacy for outdoor spaces front and back. The traditional expression of sloped roofs, covered front porches, clapboard siding, and prominent window surrounds connects the neighbourhood to the residential fabric of central St. John's. Each dwelling is made distinct from its neighbours by a range of bright saturated colours on the siding, leading to the nickname "Jellybean Row." Inspired by the house forms of old St. John's, "Jellybean Row" gave back to the city, inspiring a revival in the use of brightly painted wood in place of the near-ubiquitous ivory and beige of vinyl and aluminum siding.

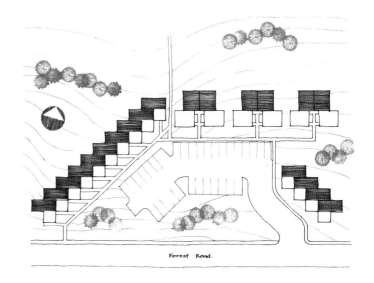

Forest Road.

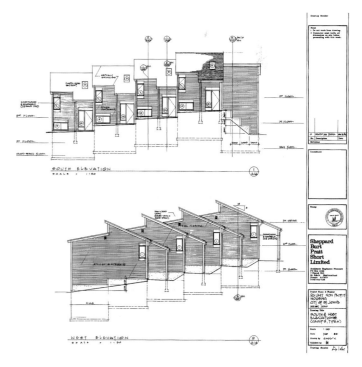

106. Detail of sequence of roofs and porch roofs of Type A units, n.d. [1983]. PHB Group collection.
107. Design Site Plan, n.d. [1980]. Marker on vellum. PHB Group collection.
108. "North and South Elevations (Group 1, Type A)" contract drawing #A6, February 1982. Delineator: J. B. Hartery. Plastic lead on mylar. PHB Group collection.

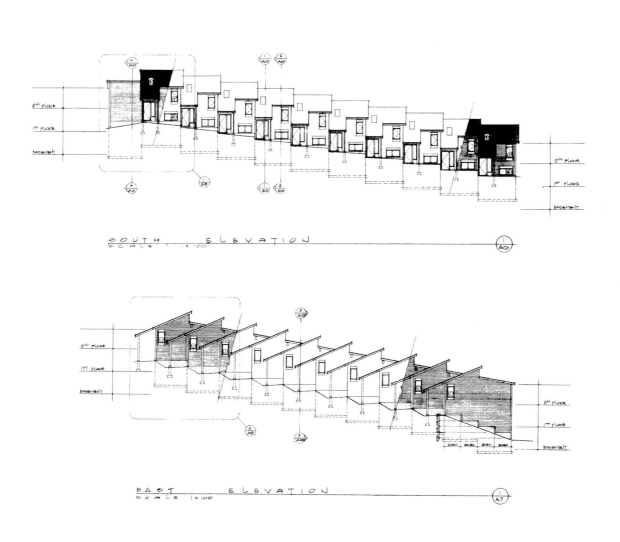

S O U T H   E L E V A T I O N
SCALE 1:100

B A S T   E L E V A T I O N
SCALE 1:100

Sheppard
Burt
Pratt
Short
Limited

Architects Engineers Planners
PO Box 6085
7 Church Hill
St. John's   Newfoundland
Canada A1C5X7
(709) 753 7158

Project Name & Number
26 UNIT NON PROFIT
HOUSING
CITY OF ST. JOHN'S
HERGRT ROAD

Drawing Title
NORTH & SOUTH
ELEVATIONS
(GROUP 1, TYPE A)

Scale   1:100
Date   FEB 82
Drawn by   J.B.HARTERY
Checked by

Drawing Number   A 14.

109. "South and West Elevations (Group 2, Type A)" contract drawing #A14, February 1982. Delineator: Carl Y. Plastic lead on mylar. PHB Group
collection.

110. Rear elevations of Type B and Type A units, facing Quidi Vidi Lake, n.d. [1983]. PHB Group collection.

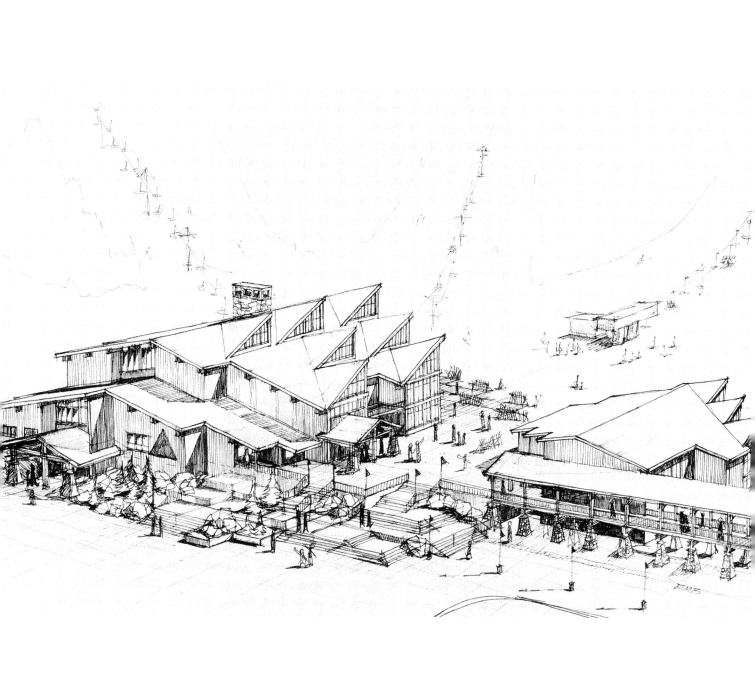

Marble Mountain Ski Lodge

1992–1996
Marble Mountain, Corner Brook, NL
Architectural firm: Byrne Architects Inc., Halifax, NS
Design architects: Michael Byrne, Gregor Byrne

Marble Mountain ski resort is located on Newfoundland's west coast, near Corner Brook. Sixteen feet of snow falls annually on the Humber Valley in the Appalachian foothills, serving a total of 31 ski and snowboard trails. The new base facilities result from a late-1980s tourism initiative by the provincial government, and are part of a master plan that includes a significant expansion of the ski facilities and a major condominium and resort development.

The base facilities comprise two shed buildings, one big and one small, separated by a large terrace and linked to the parking areas by a covered raised boardwalk. Towards the parking, the smaller building houses the ski school, children's centre, and ski shop under a gently sloping roof. The terrace acts as a staging and preparation area, with lift-ticket sales windows, trail maps and ski racks. The big shed is the lodge, seating 900 people around a two-storey mass masonry fireplace. Roof and floor beams are paired on both sides of each timber column; the dense structural grid gives the large room a forest-like spatial character. Setback edges of the upper level follow the staggered line of the tall window-wall looking onto the mountain. This serrated wall of glass is capped by a succession of half-gable rooflines, which together give a crystalline quality to the mountain facade.

111. Aerial perspective view, presentation drawing, n.d. Delineator: EMB [Michael Byrne]. Ink and wash on illustration board. Byrne Architects collection.
112. View of the lodge with Marble Mountain beyond, December 2000. Photographer: Dugal Dunbar. Byrne Architects collection.
113. Night view, n.d. Photographer: Johnathan Haywood. From Don Griffith, "Alpine Wood Architecture," Wood - le Bois, no. 16 (Winter 1996): 6. Byrne Architects collection.

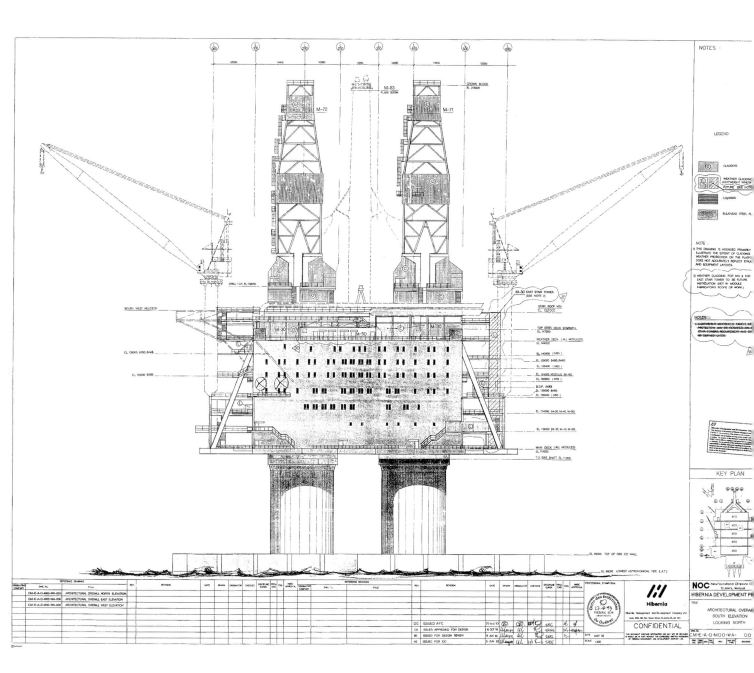

NOTES :

LEGEND

CLADDING

WEATHER CLADDING
LIGHTWEIGHT WINDSHIELD
FUTURE (SEE NOTE)

LOUVRES

BULKHEAD STEEL PLATE

NOTE :
1) THIS DRAWING IS INTENDED PRIMARILY TO
ILLUSTRATE THE EXTENT OF CLADDING AND
WEATHER PROTECTION ON THE PLATFORM.
DOES NOT ACCURATELY REFLECT STRUCTURE
AND EQUIPMENT LAYOUTS.

2) WEATHER CLADDING FOR M10 & M30
EAST STAIR TOWER TO BE FUTURE
INSTALLATION (NOT IN MODULE
FABRICATION'S SCOPE OF WORK).

HOLDS :
1) LIGHTWEIGHT WINDSHIELD PANELS WEATHER
PROTECTION MAY BE REQUIRED ON M10 & M30
EAST STAIR TOWERS REQUIREMENT AND IDENTITY
BE DEFINED LATER.

KEY PLAN

M-72   M-83 FLARE BOOM   M-71   CROWN BLOCK EL 218000

M-30 EAST STAIR TOWER (SEE NOTE 2)
STAIR ROOF M30 EL 152000

SOUTH WEST HELIDECK
TOP STEEL DECK STAIRWELL EL 147200
WEATHER DECK (ALL MODULES) EL 144060

EL 139000 (M50) (M40)   EL 140000 (M50)
                            EL 139000 (M40)
                            EL 136400 (M52)
EL 135000 (M30)   EL 134000 MODULE (M-40)
                            EL 132800 (M-40)
                            B.O.P. (M30)
                            EL 129000 (M40)
                            EL 128400 (M30)

                            EL 124000 (M-30, M-40, M-50)

                            EL 119000 (M-30, M-40, M-50)

M-30   M-50   M-30

DRILL FLR EL 156076

                            MAIN DECK (ALL MODULES) EL 114000
                            T.O GBS SHAFT EL 111200

                            EL 85000 TOP OF GBS ICE WALL

                            EL 80000 LOWEST ASTRONOMICAL TIDE (L.A.T.)

Hibernia

Hibernia Management and Development Company Ltd.
Suite 4000, 100 New Gower Street, St.John's, NF, A1C 6K3

NOC NewFoundland Offshore Construction
St.John's, Montreal

HIBERNIA DEVELOPMENT PROJECT

TITLE
ARCHITECTURAL OVERALL
SOUTH ELEVATION
LOOKING NORTH

DWG No.
CM-E-A-0-M00-WA-   00

DATE MAY 92
SCALE 1:200

REFERENCE DRAWINGS		
ARCHITECTURAL COMPANY	DWG. No.	TITLE
	CM-E-A-0-M00-WA-003	ARCHITECTURAL OVERALL NORTH ELEVATION
	CM-E-A-0-M00-WA-005	ARCHITECTURAL OVERALL EAST ELEVATION
	CM-E-A-0-M00-WA-006	ARCHITECTURAL OVERALL WEST ELEVATION

	REV	REVISION	DATE	DRAWN	ORIGINATOR	CHECKED	DISCIPLINE SUPER.	PROJ ENG.	HMDC APPROVAL
	D0	ISSUED AFC	20 AUG 93						
	C0	ISSUED APPROVED FOR DESIGN	16 OCT 92						
	B0	ISSUED FOR DESIGN REVIEW	15 JUN 92						
	A0	ISSUED FOR IDC	5 JUN 92						

Hibernia Topside Facilities: Living quarters and service module

1990–1995
Bull Arm, NL
Architectural firm: Newfoundland Offshore Contractors, St. John's, NL
Architectural firm: BFL Consultants Ltd., St. John's, NL
Design architect: Jim Case

The Hibernia Offshore production platform embodies one of the great fetishes of modern architecture, the monumentally scaled, uncompromisingly functional engineering structure. In its high degree of industrialized fabrication and modularization, and the overwhelming visual presence of the service cranes and towers, it recalls the 1960s projects of Archigram and Cedric Price. Its unsentimental approach to form and organization and its blunt readiness to encounter the extreme conditions of the North Atlantic excite the same envy in architects today that the grain elevators of Montreal and Chicago did for 1920s European architects such as Le Corbusier and Mendelsohn. Like the grain elevators, the heroic form of Hibernia that architects find so compelling is the result of the workman-like problem-solving of largely anonymous engineers, rather than the will to expression of a heroic architect.

The overall design of the Hibernia Gravity Based Structure (GBS) accommodates five huge topsides super-modules, each 18 to 20 metres wide, 84 metres long and 31.5 metres high. Four modules are devoted to aspects of oil production; the living quarters are in the fifth module, located at the south end, as far as possible from the well bay and process module. Each module was prefabricated and then transported to the shore construction facilities at Bull Arm for assembly on the topsides platform; the complete GBS was then towed to the oilfield 315 kilometres southeast of St. John's.

The work of Hibernia's architects is much finer grained and subtle than the overall form and image of the platform, but no less crucial. Weight and modularity were as crucial as cost in the development of the components, along with serviceability and safety. The 1988 Piper Alpha platform fire in the North Sea cost 167 lives; Hibernia living quarters uses a temporary safety refuge to provide two hours of fire shelter for the crew. Internally, the arrangements of the accommodation for 280 workers are designed to enhance safety as well as productivity. Containing the mud and grime of drilling and operations is one key organizational principle. Circulation routes are configured to avoid congestion and friction at critical crush areas such as the helideck, while encouraging casual interactions in accommodation and recreational areas. Natural light is maximized, and lounge and recreational spaces are distributed on each accommodation level to encourage development of smaller social units. Crew cabins are double occupancy, with separate "refuge" spaces provided outside the cabin. According to the architects, "[o]n Hibernia, these spaces are unstructured, multi-purpose spaces where 'extra-curricular' activities can flourish and personnel are free to pursue personal interests, a concept foreign to most offshore living quarters."

114. *"Architectural Overall: South Elevation Looking North." contract drawing #CM-E-A- D-M00-WAP-004, May 1992. Delineator: UL. CAD file. Hibernia Management and Development Co. collection.*
115. *(overleaf). The living quarters and service module under tow to the platform, n.d. Hibernia Management and Development Co. collection.*

Exhibition

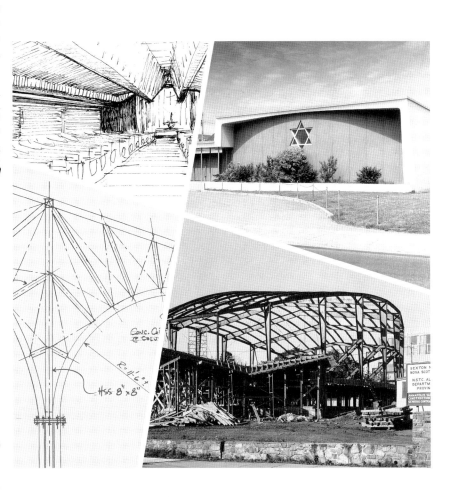

116. View of exhibition, Faculty of Architecture, Dalhousie University, Halifax, Nova Scotia, May 30 - June 20, 2001. Photographer: Ken Kam.
117. Model of curtain wall, Canada Permanent Building, Halifax, NS. Scale 1:2. Modelmakers: Ania Gudelewicz, Melanie Hayne, Darren Newton, Jennifer Uegama. Photographer: Ken Kam.

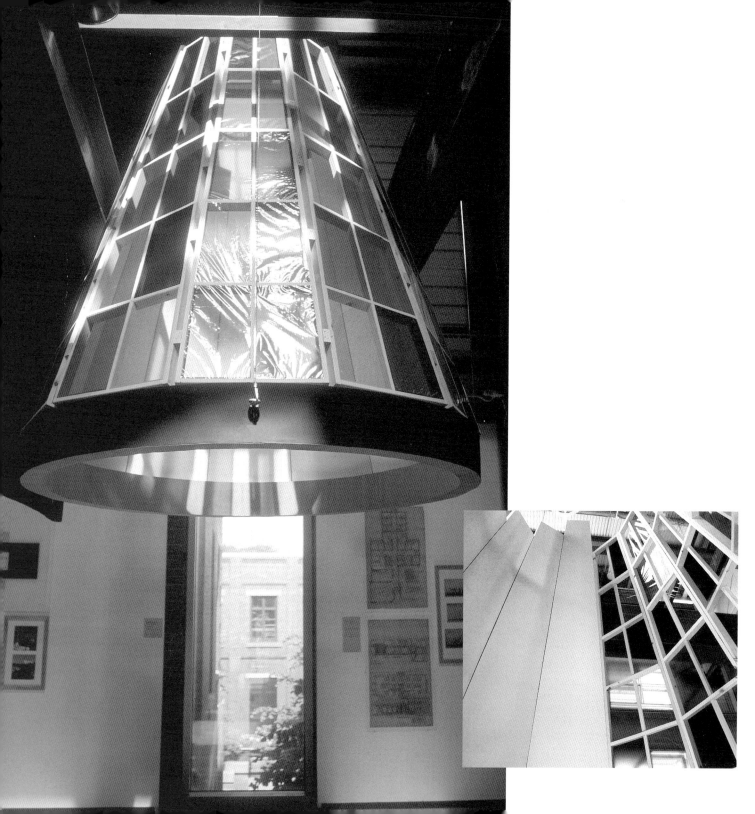

118. Model of light tower, Holy Redeemer Roman Catholic
Church, Charlottetown, PE. Scale 1:5. Modelmakers: Ania
Gudelewicz, Melanie Hayne, Darren Newton, Jennifer
Uegama. Photographer: Ken Kam.
119. Detail of model of light tower, Holy Redeemer Roman
Catholic Church, Charlottetown, PE. Scale 1:5. Modelmakers:
Ania Gudelewicz, Melanie Hayne, Darren Newton, Jennifer
Uegama. Photographer: Ken Kam.
120. Model of Beth-El Synagogue, St. John's, NL. Scale 1:50.
Modelmakers: Ania Gudelewicz, Melanie Hayne, Darren
Newton, Jennifer Uegama. Photographer: Ken Kam.
121. Rear view of model of Beth-El Synagogue, St. John's,
NL. Scale 1:50. Modelmakers: Ania Gudelewicz, Melanie
Hayne, Darren Newton, Jennifer Uegama. Photographer: Ken
Kam.

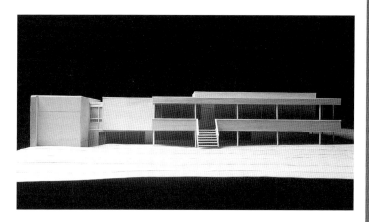

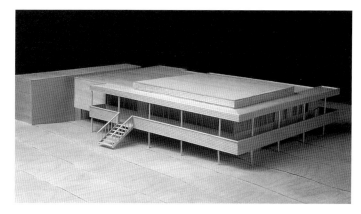

122. Front view of model of Belvedere Golf and Winter Club,
Charlottetown, PE. Scale 1:50. Modelmakers: Ania Gudelewicz, Melanie
Hayne, Darren Newton, Jennifer Uegama. Photographer: Ken Kam.
123. Model of Belvedere Golf and Winter Club. Scale 1:50.
Modelmakers: Ania Gudelewicz, Melanie Hayne, Darren Newton, Jennifer
Uegama. Photographer: Ken Kam.
124. Model of hearth of Newfoundland House, Roaches Line, NL. Scale
1:5. Modelmakers: Ania Gudelewicz, Melanie Hayne, Darren Newton,
Jennifer Uegama. Photographer: Ken Kam.

Biographies

Elide Albert
B: 1937, Caraquet, NB
Ed: BSc, Collège St. Joseph, 1958
         BArch, Université de Montréal, 1961

Sir Christopher Barlow, Bart.
B: 1929, Gosport, England
Ed: BArch, McGill University, 1953

Tom Bauld, FRAIC
B: 1924, Upper Granville, Annapolis Co., NS
Ed: BArch, University of Manitoba, 1951

David Bergmark, MRAIC, Assoc. AIA
B: 1947, Brooklyn, NY
Ed: MArch, Yale University, 1974

E. Sterling Blanchard, MRAIC
B: 1886, Charlottetown, PE.
D: 1953, Charlottetown, PE
Ed: BASc (Architecture), McGill University, 1910

Gregor Ross Byrne
B: 1962, Halifax, NS
Ed: BEDS, Technical University of Nova Scotia, 1987
         BArch, Technical University of Nova Scotia, 1991

Michael Byrne, FRAIC
B: 1937, Liverpool, NS
Ed: BArch, McGill University, 1958

Angus Campbell, MRAIC
B: 1924, St. John's, NF
D: 2001, St. Philip's, NF
Ed: apprenticed to W. J. Ryan Architect, St. Johnis NF, 1949 - 1954

Jim Case, MRAIC
B: 1958, St. John's, NF
Ed: BEDS, Technical University of Nova Scotia, 1980
         BArch, Technical University of Nova Scotia, 1981

Arthur James "Jim" Donahue
B: 1918, Regina, SK
D: 1996, Chester, NS
Ed: BArch, University of Minnesota, 1941
         MArch, Harvard University, 1942

Allan Ferguson Duffus, FRAIC, FAIA (Hon)
B: 1915, Halifax, NS
D: 1997, Waverly, NS
Ed: BArch, McGill University, 1938
         DEng (Hon), Nova Scotia Technical College, 1978

Robert Eaton, MRAIC
B: 1939, Amherst, NS
Ed: BSc, University of New Brunswick, 1960
         BArch, McGill, 1964

Charles A. E. Fowler, FRAIC
B: 1921, Halifax, NS
Ed: BSc, Dalhousie University, 1942
         BEng, McGill University, 1944
         BArch, University of Manitoba, 1948
         DEng (Hon.), Nova Scotia Technical College, 1975

Pierre Gallant, MRAIC
B: 1949, Moncton, NB
Ed: BArch, Nova Scotia Technical College, 1975

Gerald J. Gaudet, FRAIC
B: 1926, Moncton, NB
Ed: BSc, Collège de Bathurst, 1947
         BArch, McGill University, 1950

Ed Goguen
B: 1946, Minto, NB
Ed: BArch, Nova Scotia Technical College, 1970

Keith Graham, FRAIC
B: Fox Point, Cumberland Co., NS
Ed: BArch, University of Manitoba, 1950

William (Bill) Guihan
B: 1917, Sydney, NS
D: 1991, St. John's NF
Ed: BArch, McGill University, 1951

Ole Hammarlund, MRAIC
B: 1942, Copenhagen, Denmark
Ed: BArch, Massachusetts Institute of Technology, 1969

Milton Howard "Frank" Harrington, FRAIC
B: 1934, Bloomfield, NB
Ed: BArch, University of Manitoba, 1958

Alfred Hennessey, MRAIC
B: 1930, Charlottetown, PE
Ed: BArch, University of Manitoba, 1956

Peter Stephen Holtshousen, MRAIC, ARIBA, MSAIA
B: 1928, Broken Hill, Zambia
Ed: BArch (Hons), University of Cape Town (South Africa), 1958

Andris Kundzins, MRAIC
B: 1920, Riga, Latvia
Ed: DiplEng (Architecture), Carola-Wilhelmina Technical University, Braunschweig (Germany), 1947

Haralds Kundzins
B: 1898, Smiltene, Latvia
D: 1981, Halifax, NS
Ed: DiplArch, Latvian University, Riga, 1928

Pauls Kundzins
B: 1888, Smiltene, Latvia
D: 1983, Halifax, NS
Ed: DiplEng (Architecture), Riga Polytechnical Institute, 1913
        DrArch, Latvian University, Riga, 1933

Andrew "Andy" Lynch, FRAIC
B: 1944, Lunenburg, NS
Ed: BArch, Nova Scotia Technical College, 1967
        MPlan, University of Melbourne, 1968

Brian MacKay-Lyons, MRAIC, FAIA (Hon)
B: 1954, Arcadia, NS
Ed: BArch, Technical University of Nova Scotia, 1978
        MArch (Urban Design), University of California at Los Angeles, 1982

Andrew McGillivary, MRAIC
B: 1960, Berwick, NS
Ed: BEDS, Technical University of Nova Scotia, 1984
        BArch, Technical University of Nova Scotia, 1985

Junji Mikawa
B: 1934, Tokyo, Japan
Ed: BA, Tokyo University, 1956
        BTech (Architecture), Tokyo University, 1958

John Donald "J. D." Mitchell, MRAIC
B: 1921, Jeddore, NS
D: 1999, Dartmouth, NS
Ed: BArch, University of Manitoba, 1950

Keith Pickard, FRAIC
B: 1924, West Royalty, PE
D: 2001, Charlottetown, PE
Ed: BArch, McGill University, 1953

Philip Pratt, MRAIC
B: 1946, St. John's, NF
Ed: BSc, Memorial University of Newfoundland, 1967
        BArch, University of British Columbia, 1972

Henry M. Romans, FRAIC
B: 1910, Bear River NS
D: 1986
Ed: BArch, McGill University, 1937

Harold (Hank) Rounsefell
B: 1922, Halifax, NS
Ed: BEng (Mechanical), Nova Scotia Technical College, 1949

Beaton Sheppard, FRAIC
B: 1942, Indian Islands, Notre Dame Bay, NF
Ed: BArch, Nova Scotia Technical College, 1968

L. W. (Les) Single
B: 1928
Ed: BEng, Nova Scotia Technical College, 1951

Carl Smyth, MRAIC
B: 1936, Green River, NB
Ed: BArch, Nova Scotia Technical College, 1974

Anthony Staples, MRAIC
B: 1937, Bristol, England
Ed: DiplArch, Royal West of England Academy School, 1959

James F. Toombs
B: 1917, Charlottetown, PE
D: 1995, Charlottetown, PE
Ed: BArch, McGill University, 1951

Diane VanDommelen, MRAIC
B: 1959, Moncton, NB
Ed: BEDS, Technical University of Nova Scotia, 1982
        BArch, Technical University of Nova Scotia, 1984

Jeff VanDommelen
B: 1960, Wolfville, NS
Ed: BEDS, Technical University of Nova Scotia, 1982
        BArch, Technical University of Nova Scotia, 1984

Douglas Alexander Webber
B: 1901, Ship Harbour Lake, Eastern Shore, NS
D: 1971, Chester, NS
Ed: BSc (Architecture), Chicago Technical College, [before 1939]

Gordon B. Weld
B: 1932, Toronto, ON
Ed: BEng, Nova Scotia Technical College, 1955
        MScEng, Sheffield University, 1957

Acknowledgments

Nova Scotia Projects

Majida Boga
Wayde Brown, Nova Scotia Museum
George Cotaras, Fowler Bauld & Mitchell Ltd.
Trevor Davies, Brian MacKay-Lyons Architecture Urban Design
John Emmett, WHW Architects Inc.
Charles A. Fowler
Keith Graham
Frank Harrington, WHW Architects Inc.
Andris Kundzins
Brian MacKay-Lyons, Brian MacKay-Lyons Architecture Urban Design
Joylyn Marshall
Bernard Mhaladi
Junji Mikawa
Michael Moosberger, Dalhousie University Archives
Public Archives of Nova Scotia
George Rogers
Diane Scott-Stewart, Nova Scotia Association of Architects
Fred Thompson, School of Architecture, University of Waterloo
Greg Vidito, Dalhousie University Facilities Management
Roy Willwerth, Duffus Romans Kundzins Rounsefell Ltd.
Paul Wu

New Brunswick Projects

Elide Albert
Karen Chantler, Architects Association of New Brunswick
Joanne Claus, Public Relations, J. D. Irving Ltd.
Pierre Gallant, Architects Four Limited
Gerard Gaudet
Ed Goguen, Goguen and Company Ltd.
J. K. Irving, J. D. Irving Ltd.
Carl Smyth

Newfoundland Projects

Sir Christopher Barlow
David Blackmore, Director of Building and Property Management, City of St. John's
Margot Bruce-O'Connell, Hibernia Management and Development Company Ltd.
Alice Buckingham, Littledale Complex
Gregor Byrne, Byrne Architects
Angus & Maureen Campbell
Rob Campbell
Louis Cardinal, National Archives of Canada
Jim Case, Beaton Sheppard Ltd.
Centre for Newfoundland Studies, Memorial University of Newfoundland
Fiona Cuthbert, Memorial University of Newfoundland Ocean Sciences Centre
Michael Ellwood
Lynda Hayward, Newfoundland Association of Architects
Charles Henley, PHB Architects Ltd.
Peter Holtshousen

Eric Jerrett, ISR Architecture
Cassie Kent
Aidan Kiernan, Facilities Management, Memorial University of Newfoundland
William MacCallum
Robert Mellin
Helen Miller, Archivist, City of St. John's
Frank Noseworthy
Christina Parker, Christina Parker Gallery
Ned Pratt, Pratt Photography
Philip Pratt, PHB Architects Ltd.
Dale Russell-Fitzpatrick
Sadie Sellars, Hibernia Management and Development Company Ltd.
Beaton Sheppard, Beaton Sheppard Ltd.
The Sisters of Mercy
Barry Slade, Facilities Management, Memorial University of Newfoundland
William Smallwood

Prince Edward Island Projects

David Bergmark, Bergmark, Guimond, Hammarlund and Jones Architects
John Corbitt, Manager, Amalgamated Dairies Ltd.
Alfred Hennessey
Larry Jones, Bergmark, Guimond, Hammarlund and Jones Architects
Kevin MacDonald, Public Archives and Records Office, Charlottetown, PE
Alison Saunders, Amalgamated Dairies Ltd.
Charlotte Stewart, Public Archives and Records Office, Charlottetown, PE

Exhibition

Mike Archibald
Dale Arsenault, Faculty of Architecture & Planning, Dalhousie Unversity
Martha Barnstead, Faculty of Architecture & Planning, Dalhousie Unversity
Chris Bowes
Cadillac Plastics, Dartmouth
Bob Champion, Faculty of Architecture & Planning, Dalhousie Unversity
Dan Cohlmeyer
Matt Corey, Bridgeport Wire Rope & Chain, Dartmouth
East Coast Hardwood, Dartmouth
Ken Kam, Faculty of Architecture & Planning, Dalhousie Unversity
Mark MacDonald, Dalhousie University Mechanical Engineering Machine Shop
Angus MacPherson, Dalhousie University Mechanical Engineering Machine Shop
Metal Supermarkets, Dartmouth
Norman Wade Company Limited
Stephen Parcell, Faculty of Architecture & Planning, Dalhousie University
Piercey's Building Supplies
Precision Microfilming Service
Jacques Rousseau, Faculty of Architecture & Planning, Dalhousie Unversity
Troy Scott
Steve Sekerak, Faculty of Architecture & Planning, Dalhousie Unversity
Donald Westin, Tuns Press, Faculty of Architecture & Planning, Dalhousie Unversity
Melissa White

Credits and Sponsors

Curator
Steven Mannell

Assistant curator
Chad Jamieson

Research assistants
Greg Munn
Anita Regan

Modelmakers
Ania Gudelewicz
Melanie Hayne
Darren Newton
Jennifer Uegama

Steering committee
Thomas Emodi
Steven Mannell
Greg Munn
Stephen Parcell
Helen Powell
Donna Richardson

The steering committee would like to thank Kurt Forster (Canadian Centre for Architecture) for curatorial advice on the Atlantic Modern project.

Exhibition jury
George Cotaras, Nova Scotia Association of Architects
Pierre Gallant, Architects Association of New Brunswick
Larry Jones, Architects Association of Prince Edward Island
William MacCallum, Newfoundland Association of Architects
Steven Mannell, Dalhousie University Faculty of Architecture & Planning, jury chair

Sponsors
Atlantic Architects' Initiative (AAI),
    a consortium of the four Atlantic provincial architects' associations and the Dalhousie University Faculty of Architecture, funded by Human Resources Development Canada
    (sponsor for exhibition, web site and catalogue)
Royal Architectural Institute of Canada
    (sponsor for exhibition and web site)
Dalhousie University Faculty of Architecture & Planning
    (sponsor for exhibition and catalogue)
Sexton Design and Technology Library, Dalhousie University
    (sponsor for web site)
Electronic Text Centre, University of New Brunswick Libraries
    (sponsor for web site)

In memoriam

Angus Campbell

1924-2001

Keith Pickard

1924-2001

Beth-El Synagogue

1956-2001

The PEI Ark

1975-2000